To Suzy + Dave.
Love

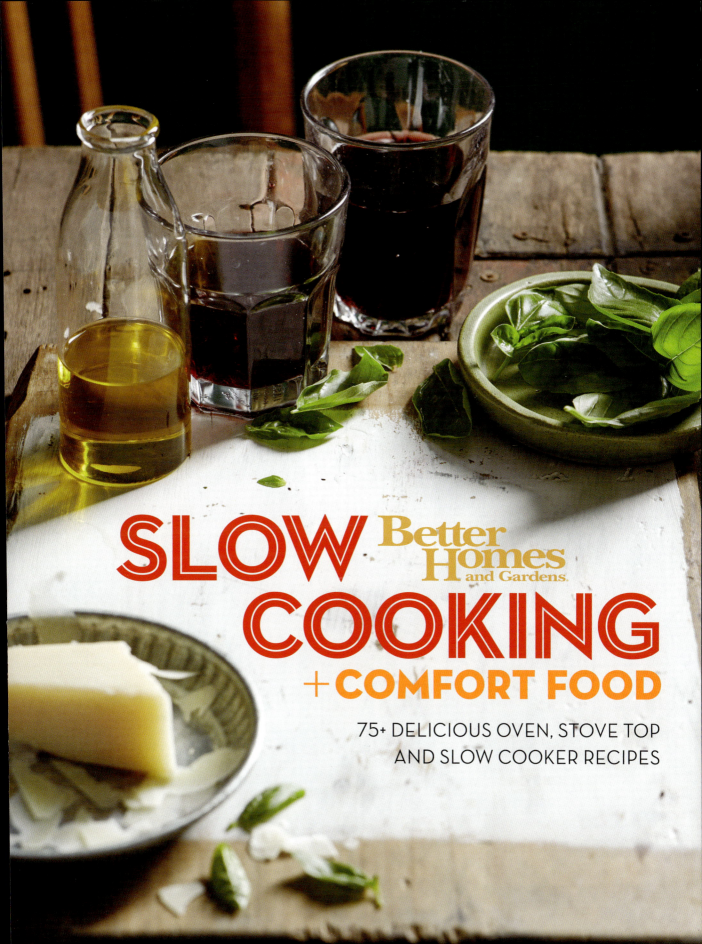

SLOW COOKING
Better Homes and Gardens
+ COMFORT FOOD

75+ DELICIOUS OVEN, STOVE TOP AND SLOW COOKER RECIPES

SLOW COOKING

Better Homes and Gardens.

+ COMFORT FOOD

75+ DELICIOUS OVEN, STOVE TOP AND SLOW COOKER RECIPES

NTENTS

Introduction **06**
Soups **08**
Chicken **42**
Lamb **64**
Pork **88**
Beef **98**
Meat-free **124**
Extras **138**
Desserts **152**
Basics **174**
Glossary **184**
Index **188**
Conversion Chart **191**

SLOW & STEADY...

Slow cooking gives us the chance to fall in love with food all over again. Low on fuss but huge on flavour, it's a chance to savour and connect, experiment and indulge, whether you yearn for comfort-food classics or prefer more modern fare. From meat-free menus and decadent desserts to saucy stews and juicy roasts, the results are impressive. And best of all, you don't even need a slow cooker for every dish. Enjoy!

Beef and dark ale stew
Recipe, page 110

soups

CHICKEN AND BORLOTTI BEAN SOUP

Check out those colours! And it tastes as good as it looks. With chicken, beans, vegies and cheese, it has all the right elements for a hearty night in!

METHOD STOVE TOP **PREP** 10 MINS PLUS COOLING **COOK** 1 HOUR 55 MINS **SERVES** 6

- 3 Tbsp extra virgin olive oil, plus extra to drizzle
- 1 cup 1cm-diced sweet potato
- 1 small carrot, sliced into 1cm-thick rounds
- 2 sticks celery, sliced into 1cm-thick pieces
- 2 cups thickly shredded green cabbage
- 1 brown onion, finely chopped
- 4 cloves garlic, smashed
- 4 rashers rindless bacon, sliced
- 6 skinless chicken thigh cutlets
- 10 whole black peppercorns
- 1 fresh bay leaf (or 2 dried)
- 6 sprigs flat-leaf parsley
- 6 sprigs oregano
- 2.25L water
- 400g can Italian cherry tomatoes in tomato juice
- 250ml red wine
- 400g can borlotti beans, drained, rinsed
- 200g silverbeet leaves, roughly shredded
- Bocconcini balls, torn into bite-sized pieces, to garnish
- Basil leaves, to garnish

STEP 1 Heat 1 Tablespoon of the oil in a large, wide heavy-based saucepan over a medium-high heat. Add sweet potato, carrot, celery, cabbage, onion, garlic and bacon. Cook, stirring occasionally, for 8 minutes, or until vegetables are just tender and bacon is lightly browned. Transfer to a bowl and set aside.

STEP 2 To same pan, add remaining oil. Once hot, add chicken and cook, turning once, for 5 minutes, or until lightly browned on the outside. (Chicken will not be cooked through at this time.)

STEP 3 Return vegetables to pan.

STEP 4 Add peppercorns, bay leaf, parsley and oregano.

STEP 5 Pour in water, cherry tomatoes in their tomato juice and red wine.

STEP 6 Cover with lid and cook over a medium heat until simmering.

STEP 7 Reduce heat to low and simmer gently, still covered, for 1½ hours, or until chicken is fall-apart tender.

STEP 8 Remove pan from heat. Remove and transfer chicken to a chopping board. Set aside for 10 minutes to cool.

STEP 9 When cool enough to handle, shred chicken meat off the bones. Discard bones.

STEP 10 Return pan to a low heat and add shredded chicken.

STEP 11 Stir in borlotti beans and silverbeet. Bring to a simmer and cook for 10 minutes.

STEP 12 Ladle soup into bowls then serve topped with bocconcini and basil.

SEAFOOD SOUP WITH HERB AND GARLIC TOASTIES

The combination of fresh seafood and fennel with sweet, zesty orange is delightful on a cool night. Use fennel fronds to garnish and add flavour. Serve with dippable toasties.

METHOD STOVE TOP **PREP** 15 MINS **COOK** 25 MINS **SERVES** 4

4 Tbsp extra virgin olive oil

12 small green king prawns, deveined, peeled, tails intact

1 brown onion, thinly sliced

1 bulb fennel, trimmed, thinly sliced, fronds reserved

3 cloves garlic, minced

1 long red chilli, seeded, thinly sliced

2 tsp dried oregano

1 tsp fennel seeds

2 Tbsp tomato paste

250ml dry white wine

400g can cherry tomatoes

500ml vegetable stock

400g skinless, boneless salmon fillets, cut into 3cm pieces

12 cleaned, ready-to-cook mussels

½ orange, cut into 4 wedges

Sea-salt flakes and freshly ground black pepper, to season

Flat-leaf parsley leaves, to garnish

HERB AND GARLIC TOASTIES

8 slices baguette

¼ clove garlic

1 Tbsp extra virgin olive oil

1 Tbsp finely chopped flat-leaf parsley leaves

Sea-salt flakes and freshly ground black pepper, to season

STEP 1 Heat ½ of the oil in a large heavy-based saucepan over a high heat. Add prawns, cooking for 2 minutes, or until lightly browned. Set aside on a plate.

STEP 2 Heat remaining oil in the same pan. Reduce heat to medium. Stir in onion, fennel, garlic, chilli, oregano and fennel seeds. Cook, stirring occasionally, for 5 minutes, or until onion is soft. Add tomato paste and wine, cooking for 2 minutes. Stir in tomatoes, stock and 500ml water. Bring to a simmer, cooking for 5 minutes.

STEP 3 Add salmon and mussels and cover partially with lid. Cook for 6 minutes (do not stir), until salmon is just firm and mussels open. Return prawns to pan, then cook for a further 1 minute. Squeeze over orange juice from wedges, then add wedges to pan and season.

STEP 4 Meanwhile, to make herb and garlic toasties, toast baguette, then rub 1 side with cut side of garlic. Drizzle toasties with oil and scatter with parsley. Season.

STEP 5 Ladle soup into serving bowls. Garnish with parsley and reserved fennel fronds. Serve with herb and garlic toasties.

CLASSIC CHICKEN SOUP

This is made for cooler days. It's nourishing and good for the soul. Eating a bowl of this is like receiving a big warm hug from someone you love!

METHOD STOVE TOP   **PREP** 10 MINS PLUS COOLING   **COOK** 2 HOURS 15 MINS   **SERVES** 4

- 3 Tbsp extra virgin olive oil
- 3 carrots, sliced into 1cm-thick rounds
- 2 sticks celery, sliced into 1cm-thick pieces
- 1 brown onion, finely chopped
- 4 cloves garlic, smashed
- 6 skinless chicken thigh cutlets
- 10 whole black peppercorns
- 1 fresh bay leaf (or 2 dried)
- 6 sprigs thyme
- 1 sprig rosemary
- 3L water
- 2 cups baby spinach leaves
- Sea-salt flakes and freshly ground black pepper, to season
- 1 handful flat-leaf parsley leaves, to garnish
- Bread rolls, to serve

STEP 1 Heat 1 Tablespoon of the oil in a large, wide heavy-based saucepan over a medium-high heat. Add carrot, celery, onion and garlic and cook, stirring occasionally, for 8 minutes, or until just tender and lightly browned. Transfer to a bowl and set aside.

STEP 2 To same pan, add remaining oil. Once hot, add chicken and cook, turning once, for 5 minutes, or until lightly browned on the outside. (Chicken will not be cooked through at this time.)

STEP 3 Return vegetables to pan.

STEP 4 Add peppercorns, bay leaf, thyme and rosemary.

STEP 5 Pour in 3 litres water.

STEP 6 Cover with lid and cook over a medium heat until simmering.

STEP 7 Reduce heat to low and simmer gently, still covered, for 1½ hours, or until chicken is fall-apart tender.

STEP 8 Remove pan from heat. Remove and transfer chicken to a chopping board. Set aside for 10 minutes to cool.

STEP 9 When cool enough to handle, shred chicken meat off the bones. Discard bones. Finely chop chicken.

STEP 10 Return pan to a low heat and add chicken.

STEP 11 Stir in baby spinach. Bring to a simmer and cook for 15 minutes.

STEP 12 Season. Ladle soup into serving bowls and garnish with flat-leaf parsley. Serve with bread rolls.

PUMPKIN, CARROT, LENTIL AND GINGER SOUP

Take the soup you know and love to healthy new heights with superfoods garlic, ginger, turmeric, yoghurt and crunchy dry-roasted almonds.

METHOD STOVE TOP **PREP** 10 MINS **COOK** 1 HOUR **SERVES** 4

- 1 brown onion, cut into thin wedges
- 2 cloves garlic, thickly sliced
- 4 carrots, halved lengthways, roughly chopped
- 6 Dutch carrots, trimmed, fronds reserved
- 300g Kent pumpkin, seeded, peeled, cut into 3cm chunks
- 2 Tbsp extra virgin olive oil
- 1 tsp ground turmeric
- Sea-salt flakes and freshly ground black pepper, to season
- 1 cup dried red lentils
- 1.5L vegetable stock
- 8 sprigs thyme
- 1½ tsp finely grated ginger
- Greek-style yoghurt, to dollop
- Dry-roasted natural almonds, roughly chopped, to serve

STEP 1 Preheat oven to 180°C fan-forced (200°C conventional). Put onion, garlic, all carrots and pumpkin on a large oven tray. Add oil and turmeric and season. Toss well to coat. Roast for 25 minutes, or until vegetables are tender and lightly browned. Set aside Dutch carrots on a plate and cover with foil to keep warm.

STEP 2 Transfer remaining roast vegetables to a large heavy-based saucepan. Add lentils, stock, thyme and ginger. Cover with a lid and bring to a simmer over a medium heat. Remove lid and cook, uncovered, for 30 minutes, or until lentils are tender.

STEP 3 Ladle soup into serving bowls. Top with a dollop of yoghurt, Dutch carrots, chopped almonds and reserved carrot fronds. Season and serve.

COOK'S TIP

Ginger is a great inclusion in a soup. Its health benefits include better digestion and detoxification.

HAM HOCK MINESTRONE

This creation is a marriage of ham hock soup and classic minestrone. Top with parmesan chips and you'll be converted to this new take on the traditional.

METHOD STOVE TOP **PREP** 15 MINS PLUS COOLING **COOK** 2 HOURS 5 MINS **SERVES** 6

- 2 Tbsp extra virgin olive oil, plus extra to drizzle
- 1 red onion, finely chopped
- 2 cloves garlic
- 1L chicken stock
- 1 ham hock
- 2 carrots, diced
- 2 sticks celery, diced
- 1 small red capsicum, diced
- 1 desiree potato, peeled, cut into 1cm cubes
- 1 swede, peeled, cut into 1cm pieces
- 400g can chopped tomatoes
- 400g can borlotti beans, drained, rinsed
- 1 zucchini, cut into 1cm cubes
- ½ cup small dried pasta (such as macaroni)
- ½ cup basil leaves
- Parmesan chips (see recipe, right), to serve

STEP 1 Heat oil in a large heavy-based saucepan over a medium heat. Add onion and garlic, cooking for 5 minutes, or until soft. Pour in stock and 2.5L hot water, and bring to a simmer. Carefully add ham hock and cook, partially covered with a lid, for 1 hour, or until meat is very tender and falling off the bone.

STEP 2 Add carrot, celery, capsicum, potato, swede, chopped tomatoes and beans. Bring to a simmer, cooking for a further 30 minutes.

STEP 3 Remove pan from heat. Remove ham hock and set aside on a chopping board for 10 minutes. When cool enough to handle, remove and discard skin. Pull ham meat off bone and shred. Discard bone.

STEP 4 Return shredded ham to pan, along with zucchini and pasta, and stir. Cook for 20 minutes, or until pasta is tender. Tear ½ half of the basil and add to soup.

STEP 5 Ladle soup into serving bowls and drizzle over the extra oil. To serve, scatter with remaining basil leaves and top each bowl with a Parmesan chip.

HOW TO MAKE
PARMESAN CHIPS

To make parmesan chips, preheat oven to 150°C fan-forced (170°C conventional). Line 2 oven trays with baking paper. Put 1 Tablespoon mounds of finely grated parmesan on prepared trays, 5cm apart. Press down with the back of a spoon to flatten slightly. Bake for 8 minutes, or until lightly golden. Set aside to cool completely and firm up on trays. Store in an airtight container for up to 3 days.

VEGETABLE AND BARLEY SOUP

Thick, rich and hearty – it's a soup you could almost eat with a fork. One thing is for sure, the pesto toasts are a must-have addition. Get dipping!

METHOD SLOW COOKER **PREP** 15 MINS **COOK** 8 HOURS **SERVES** 6

- 800g Kent pumpkin, seeded, peeled, cut into 2cm pieces
- 250g sweet potato, peeled, cut into 2cm pieces
- 2 carrots, thinly sliced
- 2 stalks celery, thinly sliced
- 1 brown onion, finely diced
- 4 cloves garlic, finely grated
- 1 cup pearl barley
- ¼ cup finely chopped flat-leaf parsley leaves
- 1 Tbsp fresh thyme leaves, plus extra to garnish
- 410g can diced tomatoes with tomato paste
- 1.5L salt-reduced vegetable stock
- 750ml water
- Sea-salt flakes and freshly ground black pepper, to season
- Basil pesto toasts (see recipe, right), to serve

STEP 1 Put all ingredients, except toasts, in the bowl of a 5.7L slow cooker.

STEP 2 Stir to roughly mix together.

STEP 3 Place bowl in appliance.

STEP 4 Cover with lid and cook on the low setting for 8 hours.

STEP 5 Remove bowl from appliance, remove lid and season. Serve soup with basil pesto toasts.

HOW TO MAKE
BASIL PESTO TOASTS
Just like the name suggests, these are super easy to make. Just toast your favourite bread and then slather on store-bought basil pesto.

CHICKEN, MISO AND SOBA NOODLE SOUP

Grab a spoon and a pair of chopsticks so you can swirl and slurp your way through noodles, mushies and chicken with Asian-inspired flavours!

METHOD STOVE TOP **PREP** 10 MINS PLUS COOLING **COOK** 2 HOURS **SERVES** 4

150g mixed mushrooms (such as shiitake, oyster and king brown)

3 Tbsp extra virgin olive oil

1 carrot, finely diced

1 stick celery, finely diced

1 brown onion, finely chopped

4 cloves garlic, smashed

6 skinless chicken thigh cutlets

1 tsp Chinese five spice

1/3 cup white miso paste (find in Asian aisle of supermarket)

3L water

150g dried soba noodles

2cm piece ginger, finely grated

2 Tbsp soy sauce

Thinly sliced long red chilli, to garnish

Black sesame seeds, to garnish

Micro herbs, to garnish

Thinly sliced green shallots, to garnish

Fried noodles (find in Asian aisle of supermarket), to garnish

STEP 1 Cut some mushrooms in half, a few into slices and leave others whole.

STEP 2 Heat 1 Tablespoon of the oil in a large, wide heavy-based saucepan over a medium-high heat. Add mushrooms, carrot, celery, onion and garlic and cook, stirring occasionally, for 8 minutes, or until just tender and lightly browned. Transfer to a bowl and set aside.

STEP 3 To same pan, add remaining oil. Once hot, add chicken and cook, turning once, for 5 minutes, or until lightly browned on the outside. (Chicken will not be cooked through at this time.)

STEP 4 Return vegetables to pan.

STEP 5 Add Chinese five spice and miso paste.

STEP 6 Pour in 3 litres of water.

STEP 7 Cover with lid and cook over a medium heat until simmering.

STEP 8 Reduce heat to low and simmer gently, still covered, for 1½ hours, or until chicken is fall-apart tender.

STEP 9 Remove pan from heat. Remove and transfer chicken to a chopping board. Set aside for 10 minutes to cool.

STEP 10 When cool enough to handle, shred chicken meat off the bones. Discard bones.

STEP 11 Return pan to a low heat and add shredded chicken.

STEP 12 Stir in noodles, ginger and soy. Bring to a simmer and cook for 10 minutes, or until noodles are tender.

STEP 13 Ladle soup into bowls. Garnish with sliced chilli, sesame seeds, micro herbs, sliced shallots and fried noodles to serve.

CHICKEN AND SWEET CORN SOUP

Oh-so-corny and damn delish, the kernels are cooked in the soup while still on the cob to give maximum sweet corn flavour.

METHOD STOVE TOP   **PREP** 10 MINS PLUS COOLING   **COOK** 2 HOURS   **SERVES** 6

3 Tbsp extra virgin olive oil

2 corn on the cob, each cut into 3 pieces

2 carrots, sliced into 1cm-thick rounds

2 sticks celery, sliced into 1cm pieces

1 brown onion, finely chopped

2 cloves garlic, smashed

6 skinless chicken thigh cutlets

10 whole black peppercorns

6 sprigs thyme

2.5L water

200ml pure cream

Sea-salt flakes and freshly ground black pepper, to season

Sour cream, to dollop

Finely chopped chives, to garnish

Crispy bacon bits (to make, see Soup toppers on page 182)

STEP 1 Heat 1 Tablespoon of the oil in a large, wide heavy-based saucepan over a medium-high heat. Add corn, carrot, celery, onion and garlic and cook, stirring occasionally, for 8 minutes, or until just tender and lightly browned. Transfer to a bowl. Set aside.

STEP 2 To same pan, add remaining oil. Once hot, add chicken and cook, turning once, for 5 minutes, or until lightly browned on the outside. (Chicken will not be cooked through at this time.)

STEP 3 Return vegetables to pan.

STEP 4 Add peppercorns and thyme.

STEP 5 Pour in 2.5 litres water.

STEP 6 Cover with lid and cook over a medium heat until simmering.

STEP 7 Reduce heat to low and simmer gently, still covered, for 1½ hours, or until chicken is fall-apart tender.

STEP 8 Remove pan from heat. Remove and transfer chicken and corn to a chopping board. Set aside for 10 minutes to cool.

STEP 9 When cool enough to handle, shred chicken meat off the bones. Discard bones. Cut kernels from corn and discard cobs. Put 1 cup of kernels in a bowl, cover and set aside for garnish.

STEP 10 Return pan to a low heat and add shredded chicken and remaining corn.

STEP 11 Stir in pure cream. Bring to a simmer and cook for 15 minutes.

STEP 12 Season. Ladle soup into serving bowls. Dollop with sour cream and serve topped with chives, bacon bits and reserved corn kernels.

SMOKY CHICKEN, CHICKPEA, TOMATO AND CHORIZO SOUP

It wouldn't be Tex-Mex without sour cream, corn chippies, avocado, coriander and, for a kick, chilli!

METHOD STOVE TOP **PREP** 10 MINS PLUS COOLING **COOK** 2 HOURS **SERVES** 4

3 Tbsp extra virgin olive oil

2 sticks celery, cut into 1cm-thick slices

1 red capsicum, diced into 1cm cubes

1 carrot, diced into 1cm cubes

1 red onion, finely chopped

2 cloves garlic, smashed

125g chorizo, finely diced

6 skinless chicken thigh cutlets

6 sprigs coriander, roots, stalks and leaves all finely chopped

1 Tbsp smoked paprika

1 tsp dried oregano

3L water

2 Tbsp tomato paste

Finely grated zest and juice of 1 lime

400g can chickpeas, drained, rinsed

Sour cream, to dollop

Dried chilli flakes, to garnish

Coriander leaves, to garnish

Natural corn chips, to garnish

Lime wedges, to serve

Avo toasts (see recipe, below), to serve

STEP 1 Heat 1 Tablespoon of the oil in a large, wide heavy-based saucepan over a medium-high heat. Add celery, capsicum, carrot, onion, garlic and chorizo. Cook, stirring occasionally, for 8 minutes, or until veg is just tender and chorizo is lightly browned. Transfer to a bowl and set aside.

STEP 2 To same pan, add remaining oil. Once hot, add chicken and cook, turning once, for 5 minutes, or until lightly browned on the outside. (Chicken will not be cooked through at this time.)

STEP 3 Return vegetables to pan.

STEP 4 Add coriander, paprika and oregano.

STEP 5 Pour in 3 litres water.

STEP 6 Cover with lid and cook over a medium heat, until simmering.

STEP 7 Reduce heat to low and simmer gently, still covered, for 1½ hours, or until chicken is fall-apart tender.

STEP 8 Remove pan from heat. Remove and transfer chicken to a chopping board. Set aside for 10 minutes to cool.

STEP 9 When cool enough to handle, shred chicken meat off the bones. Discard bones. Finely chop chicken.

STEP 10 Return pan to a low heat. Add chicken.

STEP 11 Stir in tomato paste, zest, juice and chickpeas. Bring to a simmer and cook for 15 minutes.

STEP 12 Ladle soup into serving bowls. Dollop with sour cream and garnish with chilli, coriander and corn chips. Serve with lime wedges and Avo toasts.

HOW TO MAKE
AVO TOASTS
Toast slices of sourdough bread, then drizzle with a little extra virgin olive oil and top with sliced avocado. Season and sprinkle with a pinch of dried chilli flakes for extra kick.

CHEER UP CHICKEN SOUP

It's the traditional way to fight the sniffles, but this remedy tastes amazing, too. This is the king of all healing soups!

METHOD STOVE TOP **PREP** 10 MINS PLUS COOLING **COOK** 1 HOUR AND 50 MINS **SERVES** 4

- 6 skinless chicken thigh cutlets
- 3 carrots, peeled, sliced into 1cm-thick rounds
- 2 sticks celery, stalks thinly sliced, leaves roughly chopped
- 1 brown onion, finely chopped
- 2 cloves garlic, smashed, plus extra 1 clove finely grated
- 10 black peppercorns
- 4 sprigs flat-leaf parsley, plus extra leaves to garnish
- 1 Tbsp apple cider vinegar
- 1 handful baby spinach, shredded
- Sea-salt flakes and freshly ground black pepper, to season
- ¼ cup watercress sprigs
- ½ long red chilli, thinly sliced (optional)
- Lemon wedges, to serve

STEP 1 Arrange chicken in a large, heavy-based saucepan.

STEP 2 Add carrot, celery, onion, garlic, peppercorns, parsley sprigs and apple cider vinegar.

STEP 3 Fill with water until level is 3cm above ingredients. Put lid on and bring to a simmer over a medium heat.

STEP 4 Reduce heat to low and simmer gently for 1½ hours.

STEP 5 Remove pan from heat. Remove chicken from pan and set aside on a plate for 10 minutes to cool slightly.

STEP 6 When cool enough to handle, shred meat off bones. Return pan to heat and add shredded meat to stock mixture. Stir through spinach and extra garlic and season.

STEP 7 Ladle soup into serving bowls and top with extra parsley, watercress and chilli (optional). Serve with lemon wedges on the side.

HEARTY SPICED CARROT AND LENTIL SOUP

Red lentils provide the thick base for this pot of vegie bliss. Keep it chunky or puree it smooth – it's up to you.

METHOD STOVE TOP **PREP** 10 MINS **COOK** 45 MINS **SERVES** 4

- 2 tsp cumin seeds
- 2 tsp coriander seeds
- 2 Tbsp extra virgin olive oil, plus extra to drizzle
- 2 leeks, white part only, thinly sliced
- 2 stalks celery, thinly sliced
- 6 carrots, sliced into 1cm-thick rounds
- 1 cup dried red lentils
- 1.5L vegetable stock
- ½ bunch silverbeet, trimmed, leaves thickly shredded
- Greek-style yoghurt, to dollop
- Coriander leaves, to garnish
- Lemon wedges and wholemeal bread rolls, to serve

STEP 1 Heat a large, wide heavy-based saucepan over a high heat. Add cumin and coriander seeds and cook, stirring, for 1 minute, or until lightly toasted and fragrant.

STEP 2 Add oil, leek and celery, stirring for 5 minutes, or until soft. Add carrot, lentils and stock and bring to the boil. Reduce heat to medium and simmer, stirring occasionally and skimming off any foam on the surface, for 30 minutes, or until carrot is tender.

STEP 3 Stir in silverbeet and cook for a further 5 minutes, or until silverbeet wilts. Spoon into serving bowls. Dollop with yoghurt and garnish with coriander. Serve with lemon wedges and rolls on the side.

ITALIAN BEEF AND BARLEY SOUP WITH EDIBLE PASTRY SPOONS

Forget the crusty bread on the side, this hearty beef and tomato soup is served with spoons you can eat! And they're so easy to make. Just cut out the shapes from frozen puff pastry, sprinkle with herbs and seeds, then bake. You'll never use real spoons again!

METHOD STOVE TOP **PREP** 10 MINS **COOK** 2 HOURS 15 MINUTES **SERVES** 4-6

2 Tbsp extra virgin olive oil

600g beef chuck steak, diced into 1cm pieces

2 brown onions, thinly sliced

2 cloves garlic, thinly sliced

¼ cup tomato paste

1 Tbsp roughly chopped rosemary leaves

1L salt-reduced beef stock

1L water

2 carrots, cut into 1cm dice

2 parsnips, cut into 1cm dice

2 sticks celery, thinly sliced

400g can diced tomatoes

¼ cup pearl barley

Sea-salt flakes and freshly ground black pepper, to season

Finely grated parmesan, to serve

Micro parsley leaves, to garnish

EDIBLE PASTRY SPOONS

1 sheet frozen ready-rolled puff pastry, partially thawed

1 free-range egg, lightly beaten

Sesame seeds

Dried Italian herbs

Sea-salt flakes and freshly ground black pepper, to season

STEP 1 Heat 1 Tablespoon of the oil in a large ovenproof saucepan over a medium heat. Add beef and cook, stirring occasionally, for 5 minutes, or until browned all over, but not cooked through. Remove beef from pan and set aside in a bowl.

STEP 2 Heat remaining oil in the same unwashed pan. Add onion and garlic and cook for 2 minutes, stirring. Mix in tomato paste and rosemary and pour in stock and 1 litre water. Bring to boil. Return beef to pan with carrot, parsnip and celery.

STEP 3 Stir in diced tomatoes and barley. Cover pan with a lid and cook for 2 hours, or until beef is very tender. Season and serve topped with parmesan and parsley, with pastry spoons on the side.

STEP 4 Meanwhile, for spoons, preheat oven to 180°C fan-forced (200°C conventional). Line an oven tray with baking paper.

STEP 5 Using a soup spoon as a guide, cut out 6 spoon shapes from pastry and arrange in a single layer on prepared tray. Brush pastry with a little egg, then scatter sesame seeds and herbs over the top. Season and bake for 10-15 minutes, depending on the size of your spoons, until pastry is golden. Serve with soup.

PEA, HAM AND PESTO SOUP

You can give this classic a spicy Italian flavour kick – add basil pesto to the mix, then serve the soup with chilli flakes and mascarpone instead of cream. So very yummy!

METHOD STOVE TOP **PREP** 10 MINS **COOK** 50 MINS **SERVES** 4

2 Tbsp extra virgin olive oil
1 brown onion, thinly sliced
2 stalks celery, thinly sliced
2 cloves garlic, thinly sliced
1 Tbsp oregano leaves
1 ham hock, about 800g
1 cup green split peas
1L salt-reduced chicken stock
1.25L hot water
2 cups frozen peas
60g baby spinach leaves
Sea-salt flakes and freshly ground black pepper, to season
½ cup basil pesto, to drizzle
½ cup mascarpone, to drizzle
Chilli flakes, to garnish
Basil leaves and micro herbs, to garnish
Sourdough toasts, to serve

STEP 1 Heat oil in a large heavy-based saucepan over a medium heat. Add onion and celery and cook, stirring occasionally, for 5 minutes, until onion softens. Stir in garlic and oregano and cook for a further 1 minute.

STEP 2 Add ham hock and split peas, then pour in stock and 1.25 litres hot water. Increase heat to high and bring to a simmer. Cook, stirring occasionally, for 35 minutes. Add peas and cook for 2 minutes, or until peas are tender. Mix in spinach and stir until it has wilted. Remove pan from heat and remove hock from soup, then shred the meat off the hock using 2 forks. Discard hock bone and set aside meat, covered with foil to keep warm.

STEP 3 Blend soup with a stick blender until pureed. Season, and ladle into serving bowls. Top with reserved ham meat, then drizzle with pesto and mascarpone. Scatter with chilli, basil and micro herbs to garnish, and serve with sourdough toasts on the side.

COOK'S TIP
Pesto's flavour is best when fresh, so only add it to this and other recipes just before serving to enjoy the taste hit.

OVEN-ROASTED MIDDLE EASTERN CAULIFLOWER SOUP

To make this smooth and creamy soup, you bake cauliflower and chickpeas with sumac, thyme, garlic and cumin, then blend them up and serve with pomegranate molasses and fresh mint. Wow!

METHOD STOVE TOP   **PREP** 20 MINS   **COOK** 30 MINS   **SERVES** 4

- 1kg cauliflower, cut into 5cm florets
- 400g can chickpeas, rinsed and drained
- 2 brown onions, cut into wedges
- 2 Tbsp extra virgin olive oil, plus extra 1 Tbsp
- 8 small sprigs thyme
- 2 cloves garlic, finely chopped
- 2 tsp ground cumin
- 2 tsp ground sumac, plus extra to sprinkle
- Sea-salt flakes and freshly ground black pepper, to season
- 1.25L salt-reduced chicken stock
- 2 tsp pomegranate molasses, to drizzle
- Sprigs of mint, to scatter
- Finely grated lemon zest, to sprinkle
- Lemon wedges, to serve
- Crusty bread, to serve

STEP 1 Preheat oven to 200°C fan-forced (220°C conventional). Put cauliflower, chickpeas and onion in a large roasting tray. Drizzle with oil, scatter over thyme, garlic, cumin and sumac. Season, toss well to coat, then spread out into a single layer. Roast for 25 minutes, or until cauliflower is light golden and just tender.

STEP 2 Meanwhile, pour chicken stock into a large saucepan and bring to the boil over a high heat.

STEP 3 Add all roast onion pieces, $\frac{2}{3}$ of the cauliflower and chickpeas. Reserve thyme and remaining cauliflower and chickpeas, covering with foil to keep warm.

STEP 4 Simmer for 5 minutes, then blend with a stick blender until smooth. Season. Divide soup among bowls and top with remaining cauliflower, chickpeas and thyme. Drizzle with extra oil and molasses. Scatter with mint and sprinkle with lemon zest and extra sumac. Serve with lemon wedges and crusty bread.

GINGER, CHILLI AND PORK DUMPLING SOUP

For authentic Asian flavour, make your own spicy paste with ginger, coriander and chilli as the soup base, then cheat with frozen dumplings. No one needs to know!

METHOD STOVE TOP **PREP** 10 MINS **COOK** 25 MINS **SERVES** 4

- 1 brown onion, roughly chopped
- ¼ cup roughly chopped ginger
- ¼ cup chopped coriander (a combination of roots, stalks and leaves)
- 2 long red chillies, deseeded, roughly chopped
- 2 cloves garlic
- 2 Tbsp oyster sauce
- 2 tsp sesame oil
- 2 Tbsp extra virgin olive oil, light in flavour
- 1.25L salt-reduced chicken stock
- 1.25L hot water
- 20 frozen store-bought pork dumplings
- Thinly sliced green shallots, to garnish
- Black sesame seeds and micro coriander leaves, to garnish
- Sriracha chilli sauce, to drizzle

STEP 1 Put onion, ginger, coriander, chilli, garlic, oyster sauce and sesame oil in the bowl of a food processor. Process to a coarse paste.

STEP 2 Heat olive oil in a large heavy-based saucepan over medium-high heat. Add paste and cook, stirring often, for 5 minutes, to fry and remove a little moisture. Add stock and 1.25 litres hot water. Increase heat to high and bring to boil. Drop in frozen dumplings and stir. Cook, stirring occasionally, for 10 minutes, or until dumplings are cooked.

STEP 3 Ladle dumplings and soup into bowls. Garnish with shallots, sesame seeds and micro coriander. Drizzle with chilli sauce for extra kick. Serve.

COOK'S TIP

We used pork dumplings here, but you could easily use chicken, beef or lamb varieties instead.

THAI SWEET POTATO SOUP WITH PRAWN SKEWERS

Love a curry? This spicy seafood soup is for you! With grilled prawns and noodles, it uses Malaysian curry paste and coconut milk, but you can swap for a laksa or Thai red paste.

METHOD STOVE TOP **PREP** 15 MINS **COOK** 30 MINS **SERVES** 4

- ⅓ cup Malaysian curry paste (find in Asian aisle of supermarket)
- 1 Tbsp extra virgin olive oil, plus extra 1 Tbsp
- 3 eschalots, thinly sliced
- 600g sweet potato, peeled, cut into 2cm cubes
- 2cm piece ginger, peeled, cut into matchsticks (about 1 Tbsp)
- 3 kaffir lime leaves
- 1L chicken stock
- 400ml can coconut milk
- 200g Thai flat rice noodles
- 200g sugar snaps, trimmed
- 150g button mushrooms, very thinly sliced
- Juice of 1 lime
- 1 Tbsp fish sauce
- 12 green king prawns, peeled, tails on
- Thai basil leaves, mint leaves, micro herbs and sliced green shallots, to garnish
- Lime wedges, to serve

STEP 1 Put curry paste, oil and eschalots in a large saucepan over medium heat. Cook, stirring, for 5 minutes, until eschalot slices are soft. Add sweet potato, ginger and lime leaves. Pour stock and coconut milk over, then bring to the boil. Reduce heat to medium and simmer for 15 minutes, or until sweet potato is tender.

STEP 2 Remove from heat. Use a stick blender to puree until smooth. Return to the heat and bring to a simmer.

STEP 3 Meanwhile, prepare noodles according to packet instructions, soaking in boiling water.

STEP 4 Stir sugar snaps and sliced mushrooms into pureed soup and cook for 3 minutes. Stir in noodles. Remove from heat and stir in lime juice and fish sauce.

STEP 5 Meanwhile, heat a chargrill plate over high heat. Toss prawns in extra oil, then thread onto 4 metal skewers. Grill for 2 minutes on each side, or until cooked through. Ladle soup into bowls, garnish with herbs and shallots. Top with prawn skewers and serve with lime wedges.

CHICKEN CACCIATORE

Set your drummies to bubble away in a bath of tomatoes, red wine, stock and olives for eight hours. Say no more, serve it up!

METHOD SLOW COOKER   **PREP** 15 MINS   **COOK** 8 HOURS   **SERVES** 4

---

8 chicken drumsticks

1 Tbsp extra virgin olive oil

1 brown onion, thinly sliced

3 cloves garlic, smashed

100g button mushrooms

1 sprig rosemary

1 small fresh bay leaf

250ml red wine

200ml chicken stock

400g can Italian cherry tomatoes in tomato juice

¼ cup tomato paste

½ cup whole black olives

2 anchovy fillets

2 sprigs flat-leaf parsley, plus extra to garnish

Sea-salt flakes and freshly ground black pepper, to season

Crusty bread, to serve

STEP 1 Put all ingredients, except for extra parsley, seasoning and bread, in the bowl of a 5L slow cooker (see Cook's tip, below).

STEP 2 Place bowl in appliance, cover with lid and cook on low setting for 8 hours.

STEP 3 Remove bowl from appliance, remove lid and season. Garnish with extra parsley and serve with crusty bread.

COOK'S TIP

For extra flavour, you can brown the chicken (before Step 1) in a little extra virgin olive oil in a large non-stick frying pan over a medium-high heat.

CHICKEN STEW WITH GRAPES, PINE NUTS AND AGRODOLCE

The true hero of this warming meal is agrodolce – the fiery sweet-and-sour chutney. It's sensational.

METHOD OVEN **PREP** 15 MINS **COOK** 3 HOURS 25 MINS **SERVES** 4

8 chicken thigh cutlets (bone in)

Sea-salt flakes and freshly ground black pepper, to season

2 Tbsp plain flour

3 Tbsp extra virgin olive oil

1 leek, white part only, cut into thin rounds

2 sticks celery, finely chopped

2 rashers middle bacon, finely diced

8 sprigs thyme

2 cloves garlic, crushed

Juice of 1 lemon

250ml white wine

250ml chicken stock

1 cup seedless red grapes, plus extra 1 cup

1 Tbsp pine nuts, plus extra to garnish

Baby kale, to garnish

Crusty bread, to serve

AGRODOLCE

1 long red chilli, deseeded, finely chopped (optional)

½ small red onion, very thinly sliced

½ cup red wine vinegar

½ cup honey

¼ cup sultanas

Sea-salt flakes, to season

STEP 1 Preheat oven to 140°C fan-forced (160°C conventional). Put chicken in a large bowl. Season. Add flour and toss to coat.

STEP 2 Heat 1 Tablespoon of the oil in a large heavy-based ovenproof saucepan over a medium-high heat. Add ¼ of the chicken and cook, turning occasionally, for 5 minutes, or until browned all over. Transfer to a plate and then repeat with 1 Tablespoon of the remaining oil and the remaining chicken. Set aside.

STEP 3 Heat remaining oil in same pan. Add leek, celery, bacon, thyme and garlic. Cook, stirring, for 3 minutes, or until leek softens.

STEP 4 Return browned chicken to pan. Stir in lemon juice, wine, stock, grapes and pine nuts. Bring to the boil. Cover with lid, transfer to oven and cook for 3 hours, adding extra grapes in final 20 minutes.

STEP 5 Meanwhile, put all agrodolce ingredients except salt in a small saucepan over a medium heat. Bring to a simmer and cook, simmering, for 8 minutes, or until just syrupy. Set aside to cool. Season.

STEP 6 Serve stew garnished with baby kale, agrodolce and extra pine nuts, with crusty bread on the side.

COOK'S TIP

Use ingredient swaps to play around with the taste of your agrodolce. You could use currants instead of sultanas or maple syrup instead of honey.

CHICKEN PUFF PIES

Looking for new ideas to make the most of your chicken stew leftovers? Just encase them in golden pastry, bake and share.

METHOD OVEN **PREP** 10 MINS **COOK** 20 MINS **SERVES** 4

STEP 2

STEP 3

STEP 6

STEP 4

STEP 5

Cooking oil spray

1 quantity leftover Chicken stew with grapes, pine nuts and agrodolce – with the agrodolce to serve (recipe, page 46)

2 sheets frozen ready rolled puff pastry

1 free-range egg

Sesame seeds

Flat-leaf parsley leaves, to garnish

> **COOK'S TIP**
> Steamed green beans or sautéed mushrooms taste great as a side for these pies.

STEP 1 Preheat oven to 180°C fan-forced (200°C conventional). Grease 8 holes of a 12-hole ½-cup capacity muffin tin with cooking oil spray. Measure out 4 cups of chilled Chicken stew.

STEP 2 Partially thaw puff pastry. Cut each sheet into 4 equal squares (8 in total).

STEP 3 Line 8 holes of prepared tin with pastry.

STEP 4 Spoon ½ cup of the stew into each hole.

STEP 5 Fold overhanging pastry corners into centre to partially cover filling. Pinch corners together to adhere.

STEP 6 Brush with a little beaten free-range egg yolk. Sprinkle with sesame seeds.

STEP 7 Bake for 20 minutes, or until filling is hot and pastry is golden brown. Garnish with parsley leaves. Serve with agrodolce on the side.

CHICKEN KORMA

Creamy, smooth and packed with flavour, you'll definitely need pappadums for this delicious curry to scoop up every last morsel of sauce.

METHOD SLOW COOKER **PREP** 10 MINS **COOK** 8 HOURS **SERVES** 4-6

2 red onions, cut into thin wedges

500g butternut pumpkin, seeded, peeled, chopped into 2cm dice

1kg skinless chicken thigh fillets

2cm fresh ginger, cut into matchsticks

½ cup korma curry paste

400ml can coconut milk

Sea-salt flakes and freshly ground black pepper, to serve

SERVING SUGGESTIONS

Steamed jasmine rice

Toasted flaked almonds

Pappadums

Natural yoghurt

Mango chutney

Coriander leaves

STEP 1 Put all ingredients into the bowl of a 5.7L slow cooker (as shown above).

STEP 2 Stir to roughly mix together.

STEP 3 Place bowl in appliance.

STEP 4 Cover with lid.

STEP 5 Cook on low setting for 8 hours.

STEP 6 Remove bowl from appliance, remove lid and then season to taste. Serve curry as is, or with serving suggestions, if desired.

COOK'S TIP

For an extra dose of sweetness, skip the jasmine or basmati rice and serve the korma with tasty coconut rice instead.

MEDITERRANEAN CHICKEN

Tender chicken thigh fillets are wrapped in prosciutto and simmered in a delicious concoction of tomato, oregano and olives.

METHOD OVEN **PREP** 15 MINS **COOK** 4 HOURS **SERVES** 4-6

750g baby Spud Lite potatoes

130g chilled marinated, mixed pitted olives in oil

700g jar passata with basil

¼ cup fresh oregano leaves, plus extra to garnish

1kg skinless chicken thigh fillets

100g packet thinly sliced prosciutto, halved lengthways

Sea-salt flakes and freshly ground black pepper, to taste

SERVING SUGGESTIONS

Crumbled Greek-style feta

Flat-leaf parsley leaves

Lemon wedges

STEP 1 Preheat oven to 140°C fan-forced (160°C conventional).

STEP 2 Put potatoes, marinated olives including the oil, passata and oregano in a large, wide heavy-based ovenproof saucepan. Stir to roughly mix together.

STEP 3 Wrap each piece of chicken in a piece of prosciutto and sit them on top of potato mixture in a single layer.

STEP 4 Cover pan with lid and transfer to oven. Cook for 4 hours.

STEP 5 Remove pan from oven, remove lid and season. Serve as is garnished with extra oregano and with serving suggestions, if desired.

COOK'S TIP

Nutrition note: Spud Lite potatoes have 25% less carbs than the average potato. If you can't find them, use carisma potatoes instead.

CHICKEN, CHORIZO AND BEAN CASSOULET

Spanish chorizo brings smoky, spicy flavour to this much-loved French casserole.

METHOD OVEN   **PREP** 15 MINS   **COOK** 4 HOURS   **SERVES** 4-6

- 8 skinless chicken thigh fillets, halved
- Sea-salt flakes and freshly ground black pepper, to season
- 2 Tbsp plain flour
- 2 tsp extra virgin olive oil, plus extra
- 250g chorizo, cut into 1cm-thick slices
- 250ml dry white wine
- 2 Tbsp tomato paste
- 2 tsp smoked paprika
- 500ml chicken stock
- 8 eschalots
- 3 cloves garlic, smashed
- 1 carrot, sliced into 1cm-thick rounds
- 1 stick celery, cut into 1cm-thick pieces
- 4 sprigs thyme
- 1 fresh bay leaf
- 400g tin cannellini beans, drained, rinsed

STEP 1 Preheat oven to 140°C fan-forced (160°C conventional). Put chicken in a large snap-lock bag and season generously. Add flour and shake well to coat.

STEP 2 Heat oil in a large heavy-based ovenproof lidded saucepan over a medium heat. Add chorizo and cook, stirring occasionally, for 8 minutes, or until chorizo is golden and fat rendered from it. Remove chorizo from pan and set aside on a plate, leaving oil in pan.

STEP 3 Cook chicken in batches, turning occasionally, for 5 minutes, or until golden but not cooked through. Add a little extra oil between batches, if necessary. Remove chicken and set aside on a separate plate. Add wine, tomato paste and paprika to pan and cook, stirring to incorporate anything stuck to base of pan, for 5 minutes.

STEP 4 Return chicken and chorizo to pan along with 1 cup water, stock, eschalots, garlic, carrot, celery, and herbs. Bring to a simmer, then cover with lid and transfer to oven. Cook, covered, for 3 hours, then add beans and cook for a further 30 minutes. Serve.

COOK'S TIP

You can use chickpeas instead of cannellini beans for this cassoulet, but don't be tempted to add them earlier than the recipe specifies, because they'll fall apart if cooked for too long.

CHAR SIU AND ORANGE CHICKEN POT ROAST

A twist on a favourite Chinese barbecue flavour, char siu, this tender roast chicken is a fusion explosion!

METHOD OVEN **PREP** 15 MINS **COOK** 1 HOUR 40 MINS **SERVES** 4-6

- 1.6kg whole chicken
- 20g unsalted butter, chilled, thinly sliced
- 2 thin slices orange, plus extra ½ orange cut into wedges
- 2 red onions, cut into 2cm-thick rounds
- 2 stalks celery, cut into 3cm lengths
- 2 small carrots, cut into 2cm-thick rounds
- 200g button mushrooms, halved
- 4 cloves garlic, smashed
- 2cm piece ginger, thinly sliced
- 2 star anise
- 2 tsp pink peppercorns
- 500ml chicken stock
- 250ml water
- 1 Tbsp soy sauce
- 2 Tbsp char siu sauce (find in Asian aisle of supermarket and Asian grocery stores)
- Black sesame seeds, to garnish
- Coriander sprigs, to garnish

STEP 1 Preheat oven to 160°C fan-forced (180°C conventional). Using fingertips, separate chicken skin from flesh. Insert butter and orange slices under skin.

STEP 2 In bottom of a large heavy-based ovenproof saucepan with lid, arrange onion, celery, carrot, mushroom, garlic, ginger, star anise, peppercorns and extra orange wedges. Sit whole chicken on top of vegetables and pour over stock, 250ml water and soy sauce. Cover with lid and roast for 1 hour 20 minutes.

STEP 3 Remove from oven and brush char siu sauce over chicken. Return uncovered pan to oven. Cook for 20 minutes, or until chicken is cooked through and skin is golden and sticky. To serve, garnish with sesame seeds and sprigs of coriander.

COOK'S TIP

Traditional char sui recipes use pork, but the flavours lend themselves to all kinds of dishes, including lamb, beef and tofu.

CHICKEN COOKED IN WINE WITH HERBED DUMPLINGS

The classic French dish of coq au vin becomes even more generous with this version's cheesy dumplings to mop up the juices.

METHOD OVEN **PREP** 20 MINS **COOK** 1 HOUR 50 MINS **SERVES** 6

¼ cup plain flour

Sea-salt flakes and freshly ground black pepper, to season

6 chicken Marylands

3 Tbsp extra virgin olive oil

6 eschalots

2 cloves garlic, minced

6 rashers rindless bacon, cut into 2cm strips

500ml dry white wine

250ml chicken stock

150g cup mushrooms

2 fresh bay leaves

3 sprigs thyme

DUMPLINGS

1½ cups self-raising flour

⅛ tsp sea-salt flakes

1 Tbsp finely chopped thyme leaves

30g parmesan, grated

50g unsalted butter, chilled, chopped

1 free-range egg, lightly beaten

125ml milk

STEP 1 Preheat oven to 160°C fan-forced (180°C conventional). Put flour in a large bowl and season. Add chicken pieces and toss well to coat.

STEP 2 Heat 1 Tablespoon of the oil in a large ovenproof saucepan with a lid over a medium heat. Add eschalots, garlic and bacon. Cook, stirring occasionally, for 5 minutes, or until they are golden. Set aside on a plate.

STEP 3 In same pan, heat 1 Tablespoon of the remaining oil. Add ¼ of the chicken pieces and brown, turning occasionally, for about 5 minutes, or until well browned. Transfer to a plate and then repeat with remaining oil and chicken.

STEP 4 Return browned chicken and bacon mixture to pan. Add wine, stock, mushrooms, bay leaves and thyme and bring to the boil. Cover with lid, transfer to oven and cook for 1 hour.

STEP 5 Meanwhile, to make dumplings, combine flour, salt, thyme and parmesan in a bowl. Add butter and rub in until mixture resembles breadcrumbs. Make a well in the centre and add egg and milk, stirring until just combined and a soft dough forms. Make 10 balls of dough and put on top of chicken, about 2cm apart, and cook for a further 25 minutes, or until golden and cooked through. Serve.

CHICKEN, ROSEMARY AND BARLEY STEW

The comforting flavours of barley and chicken, combined with rosemary, garlic and white wine, make this chicken dinner a winner!

METHOD OVEN **PREP** 10 MINS **COOK** 3 HOURS 15 MINS **SERVES** 4-6

8 skinless chicken thigh cutlets

Sea-salt flakes and freshly ground black pepper, to season

2 Tbsp plain flour

4 Tbsp extra virgin olive oil

2 sticks celery, finely diced

1 brown onion, finely diced

3 cloves garlic, minced

2 sprigs rosemary

1 fresh bay leaf

½ cup pearl barley

750ml chicken stock

125ml dry white wine

¼ cup tomato paste

2 desiree potatoes, cut into thin wedges

1 bunch Dutch carrots, trimmed

Steamed greens, to serve

STEP 1 Preheat oven to 140°C fan-forced (160°C conventional). Put chicken in a large snap-lock bag and season. Add flour and shake well to coat.

STEP 2 Heat 1 Tablespoon of the oil in a large heavy-based ovenproof lidded saucepan over a medium heat. Add ½ of the chicken and cook for 4 minutes, or until browned all over. Transfer to a plate. Repeat with 1 Tablespoon of the remaining oil and remaining chicken. Transfer to same plate.

STEP 3 Heat remaining oil in same pan. Add celery, onion and garlic and cook, stirring occasionally, for 5 minutes. Add rosemary, bay leaf, barley, stock, wine and tomato paste. Bring to the boil, then add potato and browned chicken. Cover with lid, transfer to oven and cook for 2 hours and 30 minutes.

STEP 4 Stir in carrots and cook, covered, for a further 30 minutes. Serve stew with steamed greens on the side.

RED CHICKEN CURRY

Forget about heading out in the cold to pick up takeaway. Start cooking in the morning and snuggle up in the evening with this easy-to-make curry.

METHOD SLOW COOKER **PREP** 10 MINS **COOK** 8 HOURS **SERVES** 6

1.5kg chicken thigh cutlets

114g can red curry paste

1 red capsicum, cut into thick strips

1 small eggplant, diced into 2cm cubes

1 carrot, sliced into 1cm-thick rounds

300g baby chat potatoes, quartered

250ml chicken stock

270ml coconut cream

Juice of 1 lime

2 tsp fish sauce

1 Tbsp brown sugar

Thai basil leaves, to garnish

Steamed rice, to serve

Lime wedges, to serve

STEP 1 Put chicken and curry paste in the bowl of a 5L slow cooker and massage to coat. Scatter vegies over chicken, then pour in stock and coconut cream. Place bowl in appliance, cover with lid and then cook on low setting for 8 hours.

STEP 2 Stir in lime juice, fish sauce and sugar. Garnish with Thai basil. Serve with rice and lime.

PRESSURE COOKER METHOD

In Step 1, put chicken and paste in the bowl of appliance and massage to coat.

In Step 2, cover with lid following instruction manual. Cook on medium setting for 25 minutes, releasing valve according to instruction manual.

LAMB

Lamb shanks with cherry tomatoes, rosemary and handkerchief pasta
Recipe, see page 66

LAMB RAGU WITH CHERRY TOMATOES, ROSEMARY AND HANDKERCHIEF PASTA

No more stirring or simmering, just pop the tomatoes, lamb, wine and herbs in a dish and roast for two hours. When your melt-in-the-mouth ragu is ready, shred the meat off the bones and toss it all with your homemade pasta. Don't forget cheese and herbs on top!

METHOD OVEN **PREP** 35 MINS PLUS 30 MINS CHILLING **COOK** 2 HOURS 5 MINS **SERVES** 4

- 2 x 400g canned cherry tomatoes
- 4 lamb shanks
- 125ml dry white wine
- 140g tub tomato paste
- 4 cloves garlic, finely grated
- 1 Tbsp extra virgin olive oil
- 3 sprigs rosemary, leaves picked (about 1 heaped Tbsp), plus extra to garnish (optional)
- 1 Tbsp dried oregano
- Sea-salt flakes and freshly ground black pepper, to season
- 300g plain flour, plus extra to dust
- Pinch fine salt
- 3 free-range eggs
- 200g fresh mozzarella, torn
- 2 Tbsp finely chopped flat-leaf parsley leaves

STEP 1 Preheat oven to 170°C fan-forced (190°C conventional).

STEP 2 To make ragu, pour tomatoes in the base of a 30cm square baking dish. Arrange lamb shanks on top. Pour over wine. Spread tomato paste over lamb, then scatter with garlic, drizzle with oil and scatter with rosemary and oregano. Season. Cover with a sheet of baking paper and cover tightly with foil so no steam can escape. Bake for 2 hours. Remove foil and use a couple of forks to shred meat off bones. Discard bones. (At this point you can serve the Lamb ragu as is.)

STEP 3 Meanwhile, to make pasta with the plain flour, fine salt and eggs, follow Steps 1-8 of the Homemade egg pasta recipe on page 148, rolling out pasta until 2-3mm thick and using a large sharp knife to cut into 25 x 7cm-wide handkerchief-looking sheets. Set aside, sprinkled with a dusting of flour so pasta strands don't stick together.

STEP 4 Just before serving, cook pasta in a large saucepan of boiling, salted water for 90 seconds, or until al dente. Use a pair of tongs to remove pasta from water and add it directly to the lamb ragu, tossing gently in sauce to coat. Serve ragu topped with mozzarella and parsley. Garnish with extra rosemary, if you like.

COOK'S TIP
If you're looking to try something new, serve the ragu with polenta instead of pasta.

SLOW-ROASTED GREEK-STYLE LAMB SHANKS

The Mediterranean flavours of lemon, garlic, feta, mint and honey turn lamb shanks into an epic masterpiece.

METHOD OVEN **PREP** 10 MINS **COOK** 3 HOURS 40 MINS **SERVES** 6

6 lamb shanks (see Cook's tip, below right)

Sea-salt flakes and freshly ground black pepper, to season

125ml white wine

2 Tbsp red wine vinegar

1 Tbsp extra virgin olive oil

1 Tbsp honey

1 lemon, halved

2 cloves garlic, minced, plus extra 4 cloves, smashed

1 Tbsp oregano leaves, plus extra ¼ cup leaves

2 tsp dried mint

500g butternut pumpkin, skin on, seeded, cut into wedges

2 red onions, cut into thin wedges

¼ cup fresh mint leaves, torn

100g Greek-style feta, diced

STEP 1 Preheat oven to 140°C fan-forced (160°C conventional). Put shanks in a large roasting pan. Season. Pour over wine, vinegar, oil and honey. Gently squeeze lemon halves over pan to release juices, then reserve. Sprinkle over minced garlic, oregano and dried mint, then rub mixture into shanks to coat.

STEP 2 Arrange pumpkin, onion, extra garlic and reserved lemon halves around lamb. Cover with a sheet of baking paper, then cover pan tightly with foil so steam doesn't escape. Roast for 3½ hours.

STEP 3 Remove foil and paper. Increase oven to 200°C fan-forced (220°C conventional). Spoon a little of the pan juices over shanks. With a ladle, transfer 1 cup of juices to a small saucepan. Return shanks to oven and roast, uncovered, for a further 8 minutes, or until golden on top.

STEP 4 Meanwhile, put saucepan over a high heat and cook for 8 minutes, or until reduced to a thick gravy.

STEP 5 Mix fresh mint, feta and extra oregano in a bowl. Season, then scatter over shanks. Serve lamb with gravy on the side.

COOK'S TIP

If you like, ask your butcher for hindquarter lamb shanks for this recipe as they are larger and meatier.

LAMB, VEGETABLE AND OLIVE STEW

Don't be fooled by the knife on the plate – cooked for eight hours, this lamb will just fall apart.

METHOD SLOW COOKER **PREP** 10 MINS **COOK** 8 HOURS 45 MINS **SERVES** 6

- 1kg boneless lamb shoulder, diced into 4cm cubes
- Sea-salt flakes and freshly ground black pepper, to season
- 1 Tbsp plain flour
- 2 Tbsp extra virgin olive oil
- 125ml white wine
- 125ml chicken stock
- 2 Tbsp red wine vinegar
- 400g (about 6) baby chat potatoes, quartered
- 2 carrots, halved lengthways, cut into 3cm-long pieces
- 1 stalk celery, cut into 2cm-long pieces
- 1 brown onion, finely diced
- 3 cloves garlic, smashed, peeled
- 5 sprigs oregano
- 5 sprigs thyme
- 250g punnet cherry tomatoes, halved
- ¾ cup pitted green olives
- ½ cup frozen peas
- ¼ cup flat-leaf parsley leaves, finely chopped
- Crusty bread, to serve

STEP 1 Put lamb in a large snap-lock bag and season. Add flour and shake well to coat.

STEP 2 Heat oil in a large frying pan over a high heat. Add lamb and cook, stirring occasionally, for 10 minutes, or until browned. Stir in wine, stock and vinegar, then bring to the boil. Cook for 5 minutes, or until liquid has reduced by half.

STEP 3 Transfer to the bowl of a 5L slow cooker and place in appliance. Stir in potato, carrot, celery, onion, garlic, oregano and thyme. Cover with lid and cook on low setting for 8 hours.

STEP 4 Stir in tomatoes, olives and peas. Increase setting to high and cook for 30 minutes, or until peas are tender. Stir in parsley and season. Serve with crusty bread.

PRESSURE COOKER METHOD

In Step 3, put ingredients in the bowl of a pressure cooker. Cover with lid according to instruction manual and cook on high setting for 30 minutes, releasing valve according to instruction manual.

In Step 4, stir in tomatoes, olives and peas and cook for a further 5 minutes, releasing valve according to instruction manual.

COOK'S TIPS

- Ask your butcher for 1kg of diced boneless lamb shoulder, or buy a whole lamb shoulder with neck meat and bones, then bone and dice it yourself. This will be the equivalent of 1kg boneless meat. Also ask your butcher for the removed bones – they're ideal for making stock.
- Adding white wine to stews creates a lighter taste sensation. Save the red to drink with it!

MASSAMAN CURRY LEG OF LAMB

It may not look like your usual Thai takeaway, but you'll love the way the curry paste flavours the lamb. Same same, but different!

METHOD OVEN **PREP** 15 MINS PLUS 15 MINS RESTING **COOK** 1 HOUR 30 MINS **SERVES** 6-8

⅓ cup Massaman curry paste

¼ cup tomato paste

1.5kg easy-carve lamb leg

800g chat potatoes

6 finger eggplants, halved

2 Tbsp extra virgin olive oil

Sea-salt flakes and freshly ground black pepper, to season

Mint and coriander leaves, to scatter

Roughly chopped roasted peanuts, to scatter

Sliced cucumber and mango chutney, to serve

STEP 1 Preheat oven to 180°C fan-forced (200°C conventional). Combine curry and tomato pastes in a small bowl. Rub mixture over lamb then put in a large roasting pan. Roast for 30 minutes.

STEP 2 Put potatoes and eggplant in a large bowl. Add oil and toss well to coat vegetables. Season, then add to pan. Roast for a further 50 minutes for medium, 1 hour for well done.

STEP 3 Remove from oven, cover loosely with foil and set aside to rest for 15 minutes. Scatter mint, coriander and peanuts and serve lamb and vegetables with cucumber and chutney on the side.

COOK'S TIP

Looking to bulk out this meal? Serve it alongside steamed jasmine or basmati rice.

MIDDLE EASTERN LAMB

Cumin and coriander are the stars of this feast. They're divine combined with sweet and succulent dried apricots. Don't forget couscous to soak up all the sauce.

METHOD STOVE TOP **PREP** 15 MINS **COOK** 1 HOUR 50 MINS **SERVES** 4-6

- ¼ cup extra virgin olive oil, plus 2 Tbsp extra
- ¼ cup ground cumin
- ¼ cup ground coriander
- Sea-salt flakes and freshly ground black pepper, to season
- 1.5kg boneless lamb neck or shoulder, diced
- 1 brown onion, roughly chopped
- 1 clove garlic, smashed
- 400g can diced tomatoes
- 500ml chicken stock
- 400g can chickpeas, drained, rinsed
- 100g baby spinach leaves
- ½ cup dried apricots, halved
- Parsley and mint leaves, to garnish
- Couscous (see tip, right), to serve

STEP 1 Put oil, cumin and coriander in a large bowl and season. Add lamb and toss to coat. Heat extra oil in a large heavy-based saucepan over a medium heat and add ½ of the lamb. Cook, stirring occasionally, for 5 minutes, or until well browned. Transfer to a plate and repeat with remaining lamb.

STEP 2 To the same pan, add onion and garlic, stirring for 5 minutes, or until onion is golden. Return lamb to pan. Add tomatoes and stock to pan. Bring to the boil then reduce heat to medium, simmering for 1 hour 30 minutes. Stir in chickpeas, spinach and apricot halves, cooking for a further 5 minutes. Garnish with parsley and mint. Serve with couscous on the side.

HOW TO MAKE
SNAZZY COUSCOUS
For fluffy, flavoursome couscous, cook it in stock rather than water. Then, just before it's time to dish it up, simply stir through chopped pistachios and chopped flat-leaf parsley leaves, season and serve. You can use pearl couscous (as pictured, opposite) or the finer traditional couscous if you prefer.

RED WINE AND CARAMELISED ONION LAMB SHANKS

Oh-so saucy and incredibly moreish thanks to your fave red wine and a li'l caramelised onion, lamb shanks have never been so deliciously easy.

METHOD SLOW COOKER **PREP** 10 MINS **COOK** 8 HOURS 30 MINS **SERVES** 4-6

- 6 lamb shanks
- 410g can finely chopped tomatoes with tomato paste
- 250ml red wine
- 250ml chicken stock
- ½ cup caramelised onion relish, plus extra to serve
- 2 bunches Dutch carrots, trimmed
- Sea-salt flakes and freshly ground black pepper, to season

SERVING SUGGESTIONS
Mashed potato
Green beans

STEP 1 Put all ingredients except carrots in the bowl of a 5.7L slow cooker.

STEP 2 Stir to roughly mix together then place bowl in appliance.

STEP 3 Cover with lid and cook on low setting for 8 hours.

STEP 4 Remove lid and add carrots. Cover with lid and cook on high for a further 30 minutes.

STEP 5 Remove bowl from appliance, remove lid and season to taste. Serve with extra relish and serving suggestions, if desired.

COOK'S TIP

You don't need to use an expensive red for this recipe, but do go for something dry like a merlot or cab sav.

LAMB WITH PEAS AND MINT

Mint sauce isn't just for serving. Instead, use it as the flavour base for this succulent lamb.

METHOD SLOW COOKER **PREP** 10 MINS **COOK** 8 HOURS 30 MINS **SERVES** 6

2 brown onions, thinly sliced
125ml dry white wine
250ml chicken stock
1.2kg boneless lamb shoulder
½ cup mint jelly
1 cup frozen peas

SERVING SUGGESTIONS
Fresh mint leaves
Mashed potato

STEP 1 Put onion, wine and stock in the bowl of a 5L slow cooker. Stir to roughly mix together.

STEP 2 Sit lamb on top.

STEP 3 Spoon mint jelly on top of lamb, spreading to coat and allowing excess to fall into bowl.

STEP 4 Place bowl in appliance. Cover with lid and cook on the low setting for 8 hours.

STEP 5 Remove lid from bowl and add peas. Cover with lid and cook for a further 30 minutes. Serve lamb with mint and potato, if desired.

COOK'S TIP
You can cook the peas in boiling water just before the lamb has finished, then stir hot peas in and serve immediately.

LEFTOVER POT PIES

Make last night's dinner tonight's winner by popping it in a pot and covering it with flaky, buttery pastry.

METHOD OVEN   **PREP** 10 MINS PLUS COOLING   **COOK** 30 MINS   **SERVES** 4

- 40g unsalted butter, chopped
- 2 Tbsp plain flour
- 200ml wine of your choice
- 200ml stock of your choice
- 6 cups leftover slow-cooked meat and/or vegetables, warmed
- 2 sheets ready rolled frozen puff pastry sheets, partially thawed
- 1 free-range egg, lightly beaten
- Sesame seeds, to sprinkle
- Freshly ground black pepper, to season
- Tomato chutney, to serve

STEP 1 Preheat oven to 180°C fan-forced (200°C conventional). Put butter and flour in a large saucepan over a medium heat and cook, stirring, for 2 minutes, or until bubbling. Add wine and stock and cook, stirring, until a thick smooth sauce forms. Add leftover meat and/or vegetables and stir until combined.

STEP 2 Spoon mixture into four 1½-cup capacity ovenproof ramekins.

STEP 3 Cut pastry into 4 pieces large enough to cover ramekins with a 1cm overhang. Put pastry pieces on top and adhere to ramekins with your fingertips.

STEP 4 Brush pastry tops with egg and scatter with sesame seeds. Bake for 20 minutes, or until golden brown. Set aside for 5 minutes to cool slightly. Season with pepper and serve with tomato chutney.

ITALIAN LAMB SHANKS WITH LENTILS

This succulent, fall-apart lamb is made wondrous with the addition of lentils and healthy vegies.

METHOD SLOW COOKER **PREP** 15 MINS **COOK** 8 HOURS **SERVES** 4-6

6 lamb shanks, trimmed
1 cup dried green lentils, rinsed under cold water
2 carrots, cut into 3cm-thick rounds
2 sticks celery, cut into 3cm lengths
1 brown onion, finely chopped
2 cloves garlic, smashed
¼ cup tomato paste
⅓ cup semi-dried tomatoes
1 sprig rosemary
1 tsp dried oregano
700ml chicken stock
200ml white wine
2 Tbsp good-quality balsamic vinegar
3 sprigs oregano
3 sprigs flat-leaf parsley, plus extra 1 Tbsp, finely chopped, and extra sprigs to garnish
Sea-salt flakes and freshly ground black pepper, to season
Steamed green beans, to serve
Bread, to serve

STEP 1 Put all ingredients except for all extra parsley, seasoning, beans and bread, in the bowl of a 5L slow cooker.

STEP 2 Place bowl in appliance, cover with lid and cook on low setting for 8 hours.

STEP 3 Remove bowl from appliance and remove lid. Season and stir in extra 1 Tbsp chopped parsley then serve topped with beans and extra sprigs of parsley, with bread on the side.

MINI LAMB SHOULDER ROASTS WITH BUTTER BEANS

This is slow cooking at its Sunday best – braise the meat and bundle a load of vegetables and beans into a heavy casserole dish. Bake for a couple of hours and then tuck in.

METHOD STOVE TOP **PREP** 20 MINS PLUS STANDING **COOK** 2 HOURS 45 MINS **SERVES** 6

- 800g deboned lamb shoulder, cut in half
- Sea-salt flakes and freshly ground black pepper, to season
- 2 Tbsp extra virgin olive oil
- 2 brown onions, thickly sliced
- 2 sticks celery, thinly sliced
- 4 cloves garlic, crushed
- 4 anchovy fillets
- 6 sprigs oregano, plus extra to garnish
- 250ml white wine
- 250g punnet baby Roma tomatoes
- 250ml chicken stock
- 40ml white wine vinegar
- 400g can butter beans, drained, rinsed
- 1 bunch Dutch carrots, trimmed, green fronds reserved
- 1 cup frozen peas

STEP 1 Preheat oven to 150°C fan-forced (170°C conventional). Season lamb pieces. Roll each piece up into a neat parcel, securing with a few pieces of kitchen twine.

STEP 2 Heat 1 Tablespoon of the oil in a large heavy-based ovenproof saucepan over a medium-high heat. Add lamb and cook, turning occasionally, for 5 minutes, or until browned all over. Set aside.

STEP 3 Put remaining oil in pan with onion, celery, garlic, anchovy fillets and oregano. Reduce heat to medium and cook, stirring, for 5 minutes, or until onion softens.

STEP 4 Pour in wine. Bring to the boil and cook for 5 minutes, or until reduced by a quarter. Add tomatoes, stock and vinegar and stir. Increase heat to high then return browned lamb to pan. Bring to a simmer, cover with a lid, transfer to oven and cook for 2 hours.

STEP 5 Remove pan from oven. Stir in butter beans and carrots. Cover and cook for a further 30 minutes. Stir in peas, cover and set aside for 10 minutes. To serve, garnish with extra oregano.

MINI LAMB POT PIES

Cooked potato gnocchi morsels make a tasty and oh-so-easy Italian-inspired pie topper.

METHOD OVEN **PREP** 10 MINS **COOK** 20 MINS **SERVES** 4

- 1 quantity Mini lamb shoulder roasts with butter beans (see recipe, page 84)
- 500g potato gnocchi, cooked
- 1 cup mozzarella
- 20g finely grated parmesan
- Fresh oregano leaves, to serve

STEP 1 Shred large pieces of meat from the Mini lamb shoulder roasts recipe into bite-size pieces. Also cut the cooked carrot from that recipe into bite-size pieces. Measure out 4 cups of mixture.

STEP 2 Preheat oven to 180°C fan-forced (200°C conventional). Spoon mixture into four 1-cup capacity ovenproof ramekins or pots. Combine cooked potato gnocchi and grated mozzarella in a large bowl. Arrange on top of lamb and top with finely grated parmesan.

STEP 3 Bake for 20 minutes, or until golden. Garnish with oregano leaves and serve.

COOK'S TIP

Instead of gnocchi, you could top the pies with a combination of mashed potato and cheese.

MEXICAN PORK WITH BEANS

This tender pork falls apart both on your plate and in your mouth. A sachet of taco seasoning and a jar of salsa are the keys to instant Tex-Mex flavour.

METHOD SLOW COOKER **PREP** 10 MINS **COOK** 8 HOURS **SERVES** 6

1.4kg piece boneless pork scotch roast

2 red onions, cut into thin wedges

500g capsicum, thickly sliced (about 3 – we used a red, yellow and green)

375g jar tomato salsa

30g sachet taco seasoning mix

400g can red kidney beans, drained

Sea-salt flakes and freshly ground black pepper, to season

SERVING SUGGESTIONS
Soft tortillas, grilled
Diced avocado
Diced tomatoes
Sour cream
Lime wedges
Sprigs of coriander

STEP 1 Put all ingredients in the bowl of a 5.7L slow cooker.

STEP 2 Stir to roughly mix together.

STEP 3 Place bowl in appliance.

STEP 4 Cover with lid.

STEP 5 Cook on the low setting for 8 hours.

STEP 6 Remove bowl from appliance, remove lid and season to taste. Serve as is, or with the serving suggestions, if desired.

COOK'S TIP

If you're looking for an alternative to red kidney beans, try borlotti or pinto beans instead.

THAI-STYLE PORK

With a can of curry paste and a couple of vegetables you'll have a meal to rival the offerings at your favourite Thai takeaway!

METHOD SLOW COOKER   **PREP** 10 MINS   **COOK** 8 HOURS   **SERVES** 6

1kg pork mince

114g can Massaman curry paste

400ml coconut milk

2 carrots, roughly chopped into 1cm pieces

2 green shallots, sliced into 2cm-long pieces, plus extra to serve

2 kaffir lime leaves, scrunched to release flavours

SERVING SUGGESTIONS

Cooked egg noodles or steamed jasmine rice

Thai basil leaves

Steamed broccolini

Lime wedges

Roasted salted peanuts

STEP 1 Put all ingredients in the bowl of a 5.7L slow cooker.

STEP 2 Stir to roughly mix together.

STEP 3 Place bowl in appliance.

STEP 4 Cover with lid.

STEP 5 Cook on the low setting for 8 hours.

STEP 6 Remove bowl from appliance, remove lid and use a wooden spoon to break the mince apart. Serve the dish as is with extra shallots and with serving suggestions, if desired.

COOK'S TIP

If you want to up the vegie count of this dish, try adding in potato, carrot and onion.

PORK SAUSAGES WITH POTATOES, ONION AND ROSEMARY

Give good old sausage casserole a sweet Italian kiss with fennel-flavoured snags, sprigs of rosemary and a tasty scattering of pistachios.

METHOD OVEN **PREP** 10 MINS **COOK** 2 HOURS 25 MINS **SERVES** 6

750g Italian pork sausages
2 Tbsp extra virgin olive oil
1 brown onion, cut into 8 wedges
2 cloves garlic, crushed
2 tsp rosemary leaves, plus extra to garnish
500g chat potatoes, halved
250ml dry white wine
250ml chicken stock
150ml pure cream
20g finely grated parmesan
Sea-salt flakes and freshly ground black pepper, to season
1 cup finely shredded silverbeet
Chopped pistachios, to serve
Creamy risotto rice (see recipe, below right), to serve

STEP 1 Preheat oven to 120°C fan-forced (140°C conventional). Remove skins from sausages and break sausage meat into 3cm pieces.

STEP 2 Heat 1 Tablespoon of the oil in a large heavy-based ovenproof lidded saucepan over a high heat. Add sausage meat and cook, turning occasionally, for 3 minutes, or until browned all over. Transfer to a plate and set aside.

STEP 3 Heat remaining oil in the same pan then reduce heat to medium. Add onion, garlic and rosemary and cook, stirring, for 5 minutes, or until onion softens. Add potato halves then pour in wine and stock.

STEP 4 Return sausage to pan. Bring to the boil. Cover with lid, transfer to oven and cook for 2 hours.

STEP 5 Remove from oven, stir in cream and parmesan. Season. Stir in silverbeet, cover and cook for a further 15 minutes. Scatter with pistachios and extra rosemary, and serve with risotto rice.

HOW TO MAKE
CREAMY RISOTTO RICE

Put 1½ cups arborio rice and 1.5L water in a large saucepan over a high heat. Bring to the boil. Cook, boiling and stirring occasionally, for 15 minutes, or until most of the water has been absorbed (should look creamy). Stir in 50g unsalted butter and 50g finely grated parmesan. Season and serve.

PORK, APPLE AND CIDER STEW WITH CRISPY POTATO

The flavours of tender pork and sweet apples combine beneath a layer of crunchy golden potato topping, just waiting to be scooped up

METHOD OVEN **PREP** 20 MINS **COOK** 3 HOURS 40 MINS **SERVES** 6

- 1.5kg pork neck, cut into 2cm pieces
- Sea-salt flakes and freshly ground black pepper, to season
- 2 Tbsp plain flour
- 2 Tbsp extra virgin olive oil
- 25g unsalted butter, chopped
- 2 cloves garlic, thinly sliced
- 1 leek, white part only, halved and thinly sliced
- 700ml dry apple cider
- 100ml chicken stock
- 200g button mushrooms
- 1 Tbsp tarragon leaves, plus extra to garnish
- 2 Granny Smith apples, peeled, cored, diced
- 400g desiree potatoes, peeled, cut into 3mm-thick slices
- 2 Tbsp panko breadcrumbs
- 2 Tbsp finely grated parmesan

STEP 1 Preheat oven to 140°C fan-forced (160°C conventional). Put pork in a large snap-lock bag and season generously. Add flour and shake well to coat.

STEP 2 Heat ½ of the extra virgin olive oil in a large heavy-based ovenproof lidded saucepan over a medium-high heat. Add ½ of the pork and cook, stirring occasionally, for 5 minutes, or until lightly browned. Set aside and repeat with remaining pork and oil.

STEP 3 Add butter, garlic and leek to same saucepan and cook, stirring occasionally, for 5 minutes, or until leek is soft.

STEP 4 Return pork to pan, then pour in cider and stock. Increase heat to high and bring to the boil. Stir in button mushrooms and tarragon. Cover with lid, transfer to oven and roast for 3 hours.

STEP 5 Stir in apple. Increase oven to 200°C fan-forced (220°C conventional). Arrange potato slices on top of pork, slightly overlapping. Brush potato with a little of the casserole liquid, then scatter over breadcrumbs and parmesan. Cook, uncovered, for a further 20 minutes, or until top is golden. Serve stew garnished with extra tarragon leaves.

> **COOK'S TIP**
>
> If you don't have access to fresh tarragon, try thyme leaves instead.

Italian beef casserole with semolina dumplings
Recipe, see page 100

ITALIAN BEEF CASSEROLE

Steak, vegies and wine cooked slow – bellissimo!
And, for a twist, try semolina dumplings on top.

METHOD OVEN | **PREP** 10 MINS | **COOK** 4 HOURS | **SERVES** 6

- 1.5kg gravy beef steak, cut into 6cm pieces
- Sea-salt flakes and freshly ground black pepper, to season
- 2 Tbsp plain flour
- 2 Tbsp extra virgin olive oil
- 2 brown onions, finely diced
- 2 carrots, cut into 2cm-thick rounds
- 750ml white wine
- ¼ cup tomato paste
- 2 cloves garlic, crushed
- 2 sprigs oregano
- 2 sprigs basil, plus extra to garnish
- 1 fresh bay leaf
- 1 Tbsp baby capers
- ½ long red chilli, deseeded, finely chopped
- 1 small red capsicum, diced into 1cm pieces
- 1 zucchini, halved lengthways, thinly sliced
- Cooked polenta, to serve
- Finely grated parmesan, to sprinkle
- Semolina dumplings (see recipe, right), optional

STEP 1 Preheat oven to 140°C fan-forced (160°C conventional). Put beef in a large bowl and season. Add flour and toss to coat.

STEP 2 Heat 1 Tablespoon of the oil in a large heavy-based ovenproof saucepan with a lid over a medium-high heat. Add ½ of the beef and cook, turning occasionally, for 5 minutes, or until browned all over. Transfer to a plate and repeat with remaining oil and beef.

STEP 3 Return beef to pan with onion and carrot. Stir in wine, tomato paste, garlic, oregano, basil, bay leaf, capers and chilli. Bring to the boil. Cover with lid and transfer to oven. Cook for 3½ hours.

STEP 4 Remove pan from oven. Stir through capsicum and zucchini. Cover and cook for a further 20 minutes.

STEP 5 Serve on a bed of polenta, sprinkled with parmesan and garnished with extra basil.

HOW TO MAKE
SEMOLINA DUMPLINGS

To top with dumplings, once casserole has been cooking for 3 hours (Step 3), begin dumplings. In a large bowl, combine 1½ cups fine semolina, 1 teaspoon baking powder, ¼ teaspoon sea-salt flakes and ⅛ teaspoon freshly ground black pepper. Make a well in centre and add 50g chilled, chopped unsalted butter and 40g finely grated parmesan. Use fingers to rub butter and parmesan into semolina mixture until it resembles wet sand. Make well in centre. Stir in 1 beaten free-range egg and 200ml milk until combined. Remove casserole from oven. Increase heat to 200°C fan-forced (220°C conventional). Stir in veg (as done in Step 4). Spoon Tablespoons of dough on top of hot casserole about 1cm apart. (Don't overcrowd dough; you may not need it all depending on width of pan.) Bake, uncovered, for 25 minutes, or until dumplings are light golden and cooked through. Garnish with grated parmesan and basil. Season and serve.

OSSO BUCO WITH FENNEL, ORANGE AND GREMOLATA

Zesty orange, fennel and a fresh herb gremolata give this Italian classic a light, fresh twist.

METHOD SLOW COOKER **PREP** 10 MINS **COOK** 8 HOURS **SERVES** 4-6

- 6 x 2cm-thick pieces veal or beef shin (also known as osso buco – buy from supermarkets or your butcher)
- 1 red onion, cut into 8 wedges
- 2 carrots, cut into 2cm-thick rounds
- 1 bulb baby fennel, thickly sliced, plus extra ½ bulb, very thinly sliced, fronds reserved to garnish
- 700ml tomato passata (strained tomato puree)
- 250ml dry white wine
- 1 Tbsp fennel seeds
- 6 sprigs thyme
- 6 sage leaves
- Finely grated zest and juice of ½ orange
- Sea-salt flakes and freshly ground black pepper, to season
- Mashed potato, to serve

GREMOLATA
- ¼ clove garlic, finely grated
- 2 Tbsp finely chopped flat-leaf parsley
- Finely grated zest of ½ lemon

STEP 1 Put veal or beef shin in the bowl of a 5L slow cooker. Top with onion, carrot and thickly sliced fennel. Pour over passata and wine. Add fennel seeds, thyme, sage and orange zest and juice.

STEP 2 Place the bowl in appliance, cover with lid and cook on low setting for 8 hours. Remove bowl from appliance, remove lid and season.

STEP 3 Meanwhile, to make gremolata, combine all ingredients in a small bowl.

STEP 4 Serve osso buco on a bed of mashed potato, topped with thinly sliced fennel, gremolata and the reserved fennel fronds.

COOK'S TIP

Got leftovers? Top slices of toasted Fresh-baked herb bread (see recipe, page 142) with reheated osso buco, scatter with a little torn fresh mozzarella, a generous grating of parmesan and a few basil leaves for an easy Sunday night dinner.

HEARTY MEAT RAGU WITH MIXED MUSHROOMS

Earthy mushrooms, rosemary and sage are the secret to this rich and robust ragu.

METHOD SLOW COOKER   **PREP** 15 MINS   **COOK** 8 HOURS   **SERVES** 6

- 1.5kg beef chuck steak, cut into 1.5cm pieces
- 250g mixed mushrooms, some whole, others halved (here, a mix of Swiss brown, enoki and wood ear)
- 1 brown onion, finely chopped
- 2 carrots, finely chopped
- 2 sticks celery, finely chopped
- 1 clove garlic, crushed
- ¼ cup tomato paste
- 250ml red wine
- 250ml beef stock
- 2 Tbsp flat-leaf parsley leaves
- 6 sage leaves
- 1 Tbsp rosemary leaves
- ¼ tsp ground nutmeg
- 1 Tbsp dried chopped porcini mushrooms
- Finely grated zest of 1 lemon
- Sea-salt flakes and freshly ground black pepper, to season
- Cooked maccheroni Calabresi pasta, to serve (or other rustic-style Italian pasta)
- Fried sage leaves (see recipe, right), to serve
- Lemon wedges, to serve

STEP 1 Put beef in the bowl of a 5L slow cooker. Top with mushrooms, onion, carrot, celery, garlic and tomato paste. Pour over wine and stock. Add herbs, nutmeg, porcini mushroom and lemon zest. Stir. Place bowl in appliance, cover with lid and cook on low setting for 8 hours.

STEP 2 Remove bowl from appliance, remove lid and season. Spoon ragu over pasta, top with fried sage leaves and serve with lemon wedges on the side.

HOW TO MAKE
FRIED SAGE LEAVES
To make fried sage leaves, heat 2 Tablespoons extra virgin olive oil in a small frying pan over a medium heat until hot. Fry 8 sage leaves at a time until crisp (about 3 seconds per side). Transfer to a plate lined with paper towelling. Set aside for 5 minutes and then serve immediately.

BEEF RAGU

The key to this thick, hearty sauce is fall-apart beef combined with tasty Italian sausage, all simmered until tender.

METHOD STOVE TOP **PREP** 10 MINS **COOK** 3 HOURS **SERVES** 6

500g beef chuck steak, cut into 3cm pieces

Sea-salt flakes and freshly ground black pepper, to season

4 Tbsp extra virgin olive oil

300g pork and fennel sausages, roughly chopped (from butchers or delis)

1 brown onion, finely diced

2 cloves garlic, finely grated

1 carrot, finely diced

1 stick celery, finely diced

1 bay leaf

250ml red wine

3 x 400g cans chopped tomatoes

¼ cup tomato paste

2 Tbsp oregano leaves

2 Tbsp roughly chopped flat-leaf parsley leaves

STEP 1 Put beef in a large bowl and season with salt. Toss well to coat.

STEP 2 Heat ½ of the oil in a large heavy-based saucepan over a medium-high heat. Add beef and cook, stirring occasionally, for 10 minutes, or until golden brown. Set beef aside, leaving oil in pan.

STEP 3 Add remaining oil to pan and heat. Add sausage and cook, stirring occasionally, for 5 minutes, or until lightly browned. Set aside, leaving oil in pan.

STEP 4 Add onion, garlic, carrot, celery and bay leaf. Cook, stirring, for 5 minutes, or until onion softens.

STEP 5 Pour in wine and cook until wine reduces by half.

STEP 6 Return browned beef and sausage pieces to pan. Stir in canned tomatoes, tomato paste and 500ml water. Bring to a simmer, then reduce heat to low and cook covered, stirring occasionally, for 2½ hours, or until beef is very tender. Season with salt and pepper then stir through herbs. For serving suggestions, see Cook's tips (below) or freeze for up to 3 months.

COOK'S TIPS

- When serving with pasta, allow 1 cup sauce to 100g cooked pasta per serve.
- Here, rigatoni was used.
- Top with extra basil leaves.

BEEF DIANE WITH MUSHROOMS AND PEPPERCORNS

Based on the pan-fried classic steak Diane, this dish is roasted for more than three hours to boost wonderful rich flavours.

METHOD OVEN **PREP** 15 MINS **COOK** 3 HOURS 20 MINS **SERVES** 6

- 3 Tbsp extra virgin olive oil
- 12 pickled onions, drained
- 2 carrots, halved lengthways, cut into 2cm-long pieces
- 1kg beef gravy steak, cut into 6cm pieces
- Sea-salt flakes and freshly ground black pepper, to season
- 2 Tbsp plain flour plus 1 Tbsp extra
- 2 cups beef stock
- ¼ cup brandy
- 8 cloves garlic, smashed, peeled
- 55g can pickled green peppercorns, drained
- 1 Tbsp Worcestershire sauce
- 2 tsp Dijon mustard
- 200g button mushrooms
- 20g unsalted butter, softened
- ½ cup flat-leaf parsley leaves, finely chopped, plus extra to garnish
- Mashed potato, to serve

STEP 1 Preheat oven to 150°C fan-forced (170°C conventional). Heat 1 Tablespoon of the oil in a large heavy-based ovenproof lidded saucepan over a medium heat. Add pickled onions and carrot and cook, stirring occasionally, for 5 minutes, or until lightly browned. Transfer to a plate.

STEP 2 Put beef in a large bowl and season. Add 2 Tablespoons flour and toss well to coat.

STEP 3 Heat 1 Tablespoon of the remaining oil in same pan. Add ½ of the beef and brown, turning occasionally, for about 5 minutes, or until browned all over. Transfer to a plate and repeat with remaining oil and beef. Return browned beef to pan. Add stock, brandy, garlic, peppercorns, Worcestershire sauce, mustard and 1 cup of water. Bring to the boil, then add browned onion and carrot, and mushrooms. Cover with lid, transfer to oven and cook for 3 hours.

STEP 4 With a slotted spoon, transfer beef and vegies to a large serving dish. Return pan to stovetop over a low heat. Combine butter and 1 Tablespoon flour in a small bowl to make a thick paste, then add to pan, stirring until it thickens. Stir in parsley. Season. Transfer sauce to a gravy boat or jug. Drizzle ½ of the sauce over beef and serve rest on the side. Garnish with parsley and serve with mash.

BEEF AND DARK ALE STEW

Got an appetite for something ale and hearty? Look no further than the aromatic flavours of this one-pot wonder.

METHOD OVEN **PREP** 10 MINS **COOK** 5 HOURS **SERVES** 4-6

2kg beef osso buco

10-12 sprigs thyme, plus extra to garnish

500g jar pickled onions, drained and rinsed under cold water

410g can diced tomatoes with tomato paste

375ml dark ale

500ml salt-reduced chicken stock

Sea-salt flakes and freshly ground black pepper, to season

SERVING SUGGESTIONS

Mashed potato

Finely chopped flat-leaf parsley leaves

Sour cream

Crusty bread rolls

STEP 1 Preheat oven to 140°C fan-forced (160°C conventional).

STEP 2 Tie each piece of osso buco with a length of twine to hold bone in place. Insert sprigs of thyme under twine.

STEP 3 Transfer to a large, wide heavy-based ovenproof saucepan.

STEP 4 Put all remaining ingredients in pan (as shown above).

STEP 5 Cover with lid and transfer to oven. Cook for 5 hours, until beef is falling apart.

STEP 6 Remove pot from oven, remove lid and season to taste. Use scissors to cut string from osso buco. Serve garnished with extra sprigs of thyme and serving suggestions, if desired.

ITALIAN BOLOGNESE

Every family's favourite, you'll be delighted with this version of the classic tomato-beef sauce after nine hours of cooking.

METHOD SLOW COOKER **PREP** 10 MINS **COOK** 9 HOURS 15 MINS **SERVES** 6

- 2 Tbsp extra virgin olive oil
- 600g beef mince
- 600g pork mince
- 1 cup red wine
- ½ cup tomato paste
- 250ml chicken stock
- 1 brown onion, finely chopped
- 2 cloves garlic, minced
- 2 sticks celery, finely chopped
- 1 carrot, diced into 1cm cubes
- 400g can chopped tomatoes
- 1 Tbsp brown sugar
- 6 basil leaves, torn
- 1 fresh bay leaf
- 1 rind of parmesan wedge (see Cook's tip, below right)
- Sea-salt flakes and freshly ground black pepper, to season
- Cooked spaghetti, to serve
- Shaved parmesan, to serve

STEP 1 Heat oil in a large frying pan over a high heat. Add all of the mince and cook, stirring every 2 minutes, for 8 minutes, or until mince is no longer red. Stir in wine and tomato paste, then bring to the boil. Cook for 5 minutes, or until wine has reduced by half.

STEP 2 Transfer to the bowl of a 5L slow cooker and place in appliance. Stir in stock, vegetables, sugar, herbs and parmesan rind. Cover with lid and cook on low setting for 9 hours. Season.

STEP 3 Transfer bolognese to a pot and serve family-style on spaghetti. Top with parmesan.

PRESSURE COOKER METHOD

In Step 1, cook minces in appliance on sauté/sear setting.

In Step 2, cover with lid following instruction manual. Cook on high setting for 45 minutes, releasing valve according to instruction manual.

COOK'S TIP

Don't toss the rind of your parmesan! It's edible and tasty. Instead, put it in a snap-lock bag and save for your next bolognese. As the sauce cooks, the rind softens and releases flavour. Lucky is the person who finds it in their bowl!

GARLIC-STUDDED BEEF IN RED WINE

Marinating is the best way to tenderise tougher cuts of meat, such as chuck steak. Soaked first in a bath of red wine, this beef will melt in your mouth.

METHOD OVEN **PREP** 20 MINS PLUS OVERNIGHT MARINATING **COOK** 3 HOURS 15 MINS **SERVES** 4-6

- 1.2kg beef chuck steak
- 4 cloves garlic, quartered, plus extra 3 cloves, smashed, peeled
- 750ml bottle red wine
- 100g speck, cut into batons
- 8 eschalots
- ¼ cup tomato paste
- 2 carrots, cut into 4cm-long pieces
- 3 sticks celery, cut into 4cm-long pieces
- 1 strip orange rind, white pith removed
- 500ml beef stock
- 5 sprigs flat-leaf parsley, plus extra to scatter
- 6 sprigs thyme
- 1 fresh bay leaf
- Sea-salt flakes and freshly ground black pepper, to season
- Mashed potato, to serve

STEP 1 Using the tip of a paring knife, make 16 x 1.5cm-deep slits all over beef (see Cook's tips, below).

STEP 2 Put 1 piece of garlic in each slit.

STEP 3 Put beef and wine in a large snap-lock bag. Seal tightly, transfer to a tray and refrigerate overnight.

STEP 4 Preheat oven to 150°C fan-forced (170°C conventional). Put speck and eschalots in a large heavy-based ovenproof lidded saucepan over a medium heat. Cook, stirring, for 5 minutes, or until browned and crispy.

STEP 5 Remove beef from bag and set aside on a plate, reserving marinade.

STEP 6 Add marinade to pan, cooking for 5 minutes, or until reduced slightly. Stir in tomato paste and bring to the boil. Add carrot, celery and orange rind.

STEP 7 Add beef, extra garlic, stock and herbs. Add water to almost cover beef. Bring to boil. Cover with lid and cook in oven for 3 hours. Put beef and veg on a large serving plate. Scatter over extra parsley. Strain pan juices through fine sieve into jug. Season. Serve beef with mash and juices.

COOK'S TIPS

• If you want to turn this into more of a casserole, dice the steak into 3cm pieces before marinating.
• Don't have time to marinate overnight? It will still taste wondrous with 4 hours of marinating.

ITALIAN BEEF SAUSAGE MACARONI

Have a delicious dinner on the table in less than an hour with this colourful mix of pantry staples and fridge basics.

METHOD STOVE TOP   **PREP** 10 MINS   **COOK** 45 MINS   **SERVES** 4-6

STEP 1

STEP 2

STEP 3

- 2 tsp extra virgin olive oil
- 650g beef sausages, chopped into 2cm pieces
- 1 red onion, finely diced
- 6 rashers rindless bacon, cut into 1cm-thick strips
- 2 Tbsp tomato paste
- 2 tsp dried Italian herbs
- 125ml dry white wine
- 2 x 410g cans cherry tomatoes in juice
- 4 cups chicken stock
- ½ green capsicum, diced
- ½ red capsicum, diced
- 1½ cups dried macaroni pasta
- 1 cup baby rocket leaves
- Shaved parmesan and basil leaves, to serve

STEP 1 Heat oil in a large, deep lidded saucepan over a medium heat. Add sausage and cook, stirring occasionally, for 8 minutes, or until lightly browned and cooked through. Set aside on a plate lined with paper towelling.

STEP 2 To the same pan, add onion and bacon. Cook, stirring occasionally, for 5 minutes, or until onion is soft. Add tomato paste, dried herbs and wine, stirring for 1 minute. Add canned tomatoes and stock and bring to the boil. Reduce heat to low, cover with lid and then simmer for 20 minutes.

STEP 3 Remove lid and stir in capsicum and macaroni. Cook, covered, stirring every 2 minutes, for 10 minutes, or until macaroni is al dente.

STEP 4 Remove pan from heat and stir in rocket. Serve with parmesan and basil.

FALL-APART GINGER BEER AND RUM BEEF RIBS

Feast on these succulent ribs inspired by the 'dark and stormy' cocktail. You won't need cutlery, but make sure there are bibs and lots of napkins handy!

METHOD SLOW COOKER **PREP** 5 MINS PLUS OVERNIGHT MARINATING **COOK** 6 HOURS 10 MINS **SERVES** 4-6

- 6 beef short ribs (about 1.5kg)
- 1 Tbsp brown sugar
- 1 Tbsp sweet smoked paprika
- 1 tsp garlic powder
- 1 tsp ground white pepper
- ½ tsp fine sea-salt flakes
- ½ tsp mustard powder
- 500ml non-alcoholic ginger beer
- ¼ cup barbecue sauce
- 2 Tbsp rum
- 1 Tbsp apple cider vinegar

STEP 1 Put ribs, sugar, paprika, garlic powder, pepper, salt and mustard powder in a large snap-lock bag. Toss to coat and refrigerate overnight.

STEP 2 Combine remaining ingredients in a large bowl or jug. Arrange ribs in the bowl of a 5L slow cooker. Pour liquid mixture over the top. Place bowl in appliance, cover with lid and cook on low setting for 6 hours.

STEP 3 Remove ribs. Pour sauce into a small saucepan and bring to the boil over a high heat. Cook, stirring, for 10 minutes, or until thickened. Brush a little sauce on ribs, then serve ribs with rest of sauce on the side. Add to rum theme with Dark and stormy punch (see recipe, below).

PRESSURE COOKER METHOD

In Step 2, put marinated ribs and sauce mixture in the bowl of a pressure cooker. Cover with lid, following instruction manual. Cook on high setting for 50 minutes, releasing valve according to instruction manual.

HOW TO MAKE A
DARK AND STORMY PUNCH

Put 4 sticks cinnamon, ½ cup caster sugar, 1 cup water and thinly sliced rounds from 1 orange in a medium saucepan and bring to the boil over a high heat. Boil for 2 minutes, or until sugar has dissolved. Remove from heat and set aside for 15 minutes. Transfer syrup to a jug and put in refrigerator for 30 minutes, or until cold. Remove and discard orange slices and cinnamon sticks. Put cooled syrup, thinly sliced rounds from 1 lemon, ½ cup dark rum, 125g fresh raspberries and thinly sliced rounds from another orange in a large serving jug. Pour in 1.25L ginger ale and top up with ice cubes. Serve punch garnished with extra sticks of cinnamon.

BEEF IN GUINNESS

Think beef and Guinness pie without having to fiddle with pastry.
You won't miss it, either, with nutty, earthy parsnips mixed through.

METHOD OVEN **PREP** 20 MINS **COOK** 2 HOURS **SERVES** 6

- 1.5kg beef chuck steak, excess fat trimmed, cut into 3cm pieces
- Sea-salt flakes and freshly ground black pepper, to season
- ¼ cup plain flour
- ¼ cup extra virgin olive oil
- 4 brown onions, cut into wedges
- ¼ cup thyme leaves
- 500ml Guinness stout
- 250ml beef stock
- ¼ cup tomato paste
- 60ml Worcestershire sauce
- 4 small parsnips, peeled, trimmed, quartered
- Mashed potato, to serve (optional)

STEP 1 Preheat oven to 180°C fan-forced (200°C conventional). Put beef in a large bowl and season well. Add flour and toss to coat.

STEP 2 Heat 1 Tablespoon of the oil in a large ovenproof saucepan with lid over a medium heat. Add ½ of the beef, turning occasionally, for about 5 minutes, or until browned. Transfer to a plate and repeat with 1 Tablespoon of the remaining oil and all remaining beef. Set aside on plate.

STEP 3 To same pan, add all remaining oil and onion. Cook, stirring occasionally, for 5 minutes, or until lightly browned.

STEP 4 Return beef to pan with thyme, Guinness, stock, paste and Worcestershire sauce. Increase heat to high and bring to the boil. Cover with lid and cook in oven for 1 hour, or until meat is tender. Add parsnip and cook for a further 45 minutes. Serve with mashed potato, if desired.

COOK'S TIP

Add some colour to your dish with a side of creamy mashed sweet potato. Delish!

BEEF, RICOTTA AND SPINACH LASAGNE

Lasagne in a slow cooker? It's not only possible, it's remarkably easy and tastes absolutely amazing. Go on, give it a go!

METHOD SLOW COOKER   **PREP** 15 MINS PLUS SETTING   **COOK** 4 HOURS   **SERVES** 6–8

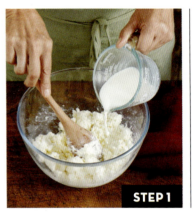
STEP 1

STEP 3

STEP 5

500g fresh ricotta

½ cup milk

¼ cup finely grated parmesan

10 grates of 1 whole nutmeg

Sea-salt flakes and freshly ground black pepper, to season

6 cups cooked Italian bolognese (see recipe, page 112), chilled

2 cups shredded mozzarella

4 sheets (from 375g packet) large instant dried lasagne

50g baby spinach leaves

Basil leaves, to garnish

STEP 1 Combine ricotta, milk, parmesan and nutmeg in a large bowl and season.

STEP 2 Spoon ⅓ of the bolognese into the bowl of a 5L slow cooker, spreading to cover base.

STEP 3 Top with ⅓ of the ricotta mixture, spreading to cover bolognese. Scatter over ½ cup of the mozzarella.

STEP 4 Using 2 lasagne sheets, cover mozzarella layer with a single layer of lasagne sheets, broken into pieces as necessary to fit snugly in bowl.

STEP 5 Top with ½ of the spinach.

STEP 6 Repeat Steps 2–5 to make another layer, then finish layering with remaining ⅓ of the bolognese, remaining ⅓ of the ricotta mixture and remaining 1 cup of the mozzarella. Place bowl in appliance, put lid on and cook on low setting for 4 hours.

STEP 7 Remove bowl from appliance, remove lid and set aside for 15 minutes to allow juices to settle.

STEP 8 Serve lasagne garnished with basil and freshly ground black pepper.

CHILLI CON LENTIL STUFFED CAPSICUMS

Slow cooking isn't just for stews. Feast your eyes on this colourful Mexican snack. And don't skimp on the crunchy corn chips!

METHOD OVEN **PREP** 15 MINS **COOK** 2 HOURS 45 MINS **SERVES** 6

- 3 red capsicums, halved lengthways
- 500g tomato, onion and garlic pasta sauce
- 2 Tbsp extra virgin olive oil
- 1 brown onion, finely diced
- 2 cloves garlic, minced
- 2 tsp ground cumin
- 1 tsp ground cinnamon
- ½ tsp ground chilli
- 1 tsp dried oregano
- ½ bunch coriander, leaves picked, stalks washed and finely chopped
- 400g can brown lentils, drained, rinsed
- 400g can red kidney beans, drained, rinsed
- 400g can chopped tomatoes
- 125ml vegetable stock
- 200g sweet potato, peeled, diced into 1cm cubes
- Sea-salt flakes and freshly ground black pepper, to season
- ½ cup shredded tasty cheese
- 12 slices sourdough, toasted
- Sour cream, to top
- Diced avocado, to top
- Corn chips, to top

STEP 1 Using a teaspoon, remove and discard seeds and white membrane from inside capsicum halves. Pour pasta sauce into base of a large roasting pan, then arrange capsicum halves, cut-side up, in sauce.

STEP 2 Heat oil in a large heavy-based saucepan over a medium heat. Add onion and garlic and cook for 2 minutes. Add cumin, cinnamon, chilli, oregano and coriander stalks and cook, stirring, for 1 minute, or until fragrant. Add lentils, beans, chopped tomatoes and stock and bring to the boil. Stir in sweet potato. Remove pan from heat and season.

STEP 3 Preheat oven to 120°C fan-forced (140°C conventional). Spoon hot mixture into capsicum halves. Cover roasting pan with baking paper then wrap tightly with foil and roast for 2 hours 30 minutes. Remove foil and baking paper and scatter cheese over capsicum. Increase oven to 200°C fan-forced (220°C conventional) and roast for a further 5 minutes, or until cheese has melted. Serve each capsicum half on 2 slices of sourdough topped with sour cream, avocado, corn chips and coriander leaves.

MUSHROOM AND LENTIL RAGU

A meat-free ragu, served with all the bells and whistles – fettuccine, fresh herbs and lots of grated parmesan.

METHOD OVEN **PREP** 20 MINS **COOK** 3 HOURS **SERVES** 4-6

- 1kg mixed mushrooms (we used flat, portobello, Swiss brown and button)
- 1 cup whole green lentils
- 1 brown onion, finely chopped
- 4 sticks celery, finely chopped
- 3 cloves garlic, crushed
- ½ cup tomato paste
- 400g can diced tomatoes
- 400ml red wine
- 300ml vegetable stock
- 3 Tbsp extra virgin olive oil
- ¼ cup roughly chopped flat-leaf parsley leaves, plus extra to garnish
- 1 Tbsp chopped rosemary leaves
- ¼ tsp ground nutmeg
- 20g parmesan, roughly chopped, plus extra finely shaved to serve
- Sea-salt flakes and freshly ground black pepper, to season
- Cooked fettuccine pasta, to serve

STEP 1 Preheat oven to 140°C fan-forced (160°C conventional). Roughly chop large mushrooms, quarter medium mushrooms and leave small mushrooms whole. Transfer into the bowl of a 3.8L wide cast-iron saucepan.

STEP 2 Top with lentils, vegetables, garlic, tomato paste, tomatoes, wine, stock, oil, herbs, nutmeg and parmesan. Stir to roughly mix together. Cover with lid and bake for 3 hours.

STEP 3 Season and serve with pasta and extra shaved parmesan, garnished with extra parsley.

IN THE SLOW COOKER

STEP 1 Roughly chop large mushrooms and halve smaller mushrooms, then transfer to the bowl of a 5L slow cooker. Top with lentils, vegetables, garlic, tomato paste, tomatoes, wine, stock, oil, herbs, nutmeg and parmesan.

STEP 2 Stir to roughly mix together then place bowl in appliance. Cover with lid and cook on the low setting for 8 hours.

STEP 3 Remove bowl from appliance, remove lid and season. Serve with pasta and extra parmesan, and garnish with extra parsley.

COOK'S TIP

To make this dish gluten-free, you could serve it with soft polenta instead of fettuccine.

RICOTTA, PESTO AND BROWN RICE STUFFED CAPSICUMS

The nutty brown rice filling is flavoured with a classic Italian flavour combo. Don't forget the fresh basil to serve – yum!

METHOD SLOW COOKER **PREP** 15 MINS **COOK** 6 HOURS **SERVES** 6

- 6 small red capsicums
- 2 x 250g packets microwave brown rice (not heated)
- 375g smooth ricotta
- 2 Tbsp dried Italian herbs
- ¼ cup basil leaves, finely chopped, plus extra to serve
- 4 green shallots, thinly sliced
- 50g parmesan, finely grated, plus extra to serve
- 190g jar basil pesto
- Sea-salt flakes and freshly ground black pepper, to season
- 700ml tomato-based pasta sauce

STEP 1 Cut off, and reserve, tops of capsicums. With your hand, remove and discard white membrane and seeds from inside each capsicum.

STEP 2 Combine rice, ricotta, dried herbs, basil, shallots and parmesan in a large bowl, then stir in ¼ cup of the pesto. Season.

STEP 3 Pour pasta sauce into the bowl of a 5L slow cooker. Put capsicums in sauce, open-side up, so they sit snuggly. Spoon rice mixture evenly into capsicums, then cover with reserved capsicum tops.

STEP 4 Cover with lid and cook on the low setting for 6 hours.

STEP 5 Remove bowl from appliance and remove lid. Serve the capsicums garnished with extra basil, with extra parmesan and remaining pesto on the side to add as desired.

COOK'S TIPS

- You can substitute microwave white rice for the brown rice.
- Purchase ricotta from the deli, instead of in a tub, as it's firmer and less wet than the pre-packaged types.

LENTIL AND EGGPLANT RAGU

Left to cook for just over six hours, this pasta sauce is easy to make.
Just fry the veg then throw it all in your slow cooker to bubble away.

METHOD SLOW COOKER **PREP** 10 MINS **COOK** 6 HOURS 20 MINS **SERVES** 6

2 Tbsp extra virgin olive oil
1 brown onion, finely chopped
2 cloves garlic, minced
2 sticks celery, finely chopped
1 carrot, sliced into 1cm-thick rounds
1 eggplant, diced into 1cm cubes
1 cup red wine
½ cup tomato paste
750ml vegetable stock
375g pack whole green lentils, rinsed
400g can chopped tomatoes
6 basil leaves, torn, plus extra to serve
1 fresh bay leaf
1 Tbsp balsamic vinegar
1 Tbsp brown sugar
Sea-salt flakes and freshly ground black pepper, to season
Cooked penne, to serve
Shaved parmesan, to serve

STEP 1 Heat oil in a large frying pan over a high heat. Add onion, garlic, celery and carrot and cook, stirring occasionally, for 5 minutes, or until lightly browned. Add eggplant and cook for a further 5 minutes, or until eggplant has softened slightly. Stir in wine and tomato paste, then bring to the boil. Cook for 5 minutes, or until wine has reduced by half. Transfer mixture to the bowl of a 5L slow cooker and place in appliance.

STEP 2 Stir in 2 cups of water, stock, lentils, tomatoes, herbs, ½ of the vinegar and ½ of the sugar. Cover with lid and cook on low setting for 6 hours. Stir in remaining vinegar and remaining sugar. Season.

STEP 3 Serve lentil and eggplant ragu on, or tossed through, cooked penne. Scatter over shaved parmesan and extra basil leaves.

> **COOK'S TIPS**
> • If you don't have any penne in the cupboard, use another tube-shaped pasta, such as ziti, rigatoni or macaroni, as these shapes work best with hearty sauces such as ragus.
> • For a dash of crunch to offset the beautiful softness of the lentils and eggplant, you could add some chopped walnuts to this dish to serve.

MIDDLE EASTERN EGGPLANTS

Smother eggplants in a spiced tomato paste, then slow cook for hours until they fall apart.

METHOD OVEN   **PREP** 15 MINS   **COOK** 4 HOURS   **SERVES** 4-6

- ¼ cup tomato paste
- 1 Tbsp honey
- 1 tsp sumac
- 1 tsp dried oregano
- 1 tsp ground coriander
- 1 tsp ground cumin
- ½ tsp sea-salt flakes, plus extra to season
- 3 medium eggplants, tops trimmed, halved lengthways
- 3 Tbsp extra virgin olive oil
- 150ml white wine
- 1 red onion, sliced into thin rounds
- 2 tomatoes, finely diced
- Freshly ground black pepper, to season
- ½ cup Greek-style yoghurt, to dollop
- 1 tsp pomegranate molasses, to dollop
- Roughly chopped walnuts, to scatter
- Mint leaves, to scatter
- Pomegranate arils (seeds), to scatter
- Lemon wedges, to serve
- Couscous, to serve

STEP 1 Preheat oven to 140°C fan-forced (160°C conventional). Combine tomato paste, honey, sumac, oregano, coriander, cumin and salt in a small bowl.

STEP 2 Use a small sharp knife to cut a criss-cross pattern into eggplant halves, without cutting all the way through the skin. Arrange eggplant halves in a 30 x 40cm baking dish, cut-side up. Drizzle with oil.

STEP 3 Spoon tomato paste mixture on top of eggplant halves and then use a teaspoon to push the mixture down into the cuts.

STEP 4 Drizzle over wine, spoon onion and tomato on top of eggplant and season. Cover with a sheet of baking paper, then cover tightly with foil to ensure no steam can escape. Bake for 4 hours.

STEP 5 Remove dish from oven and remove foil and baking paper. Dollop with yoghurt and pomegranate molasses, and scatter with walnuts, mint and pomegranate arils. Serve with lemon wedges and couscous on the side.

SPINACH AND RICOTTA CANNELLONI

Vegetarians delight! This family favourite is a breeze to cook, using just a handful of simple, top-quality ingredients.

METHOD SLOW COOKER **PREP** 30 MINS **COOK** 2 HOURS 50 MINS **SERVES** 4

STEP 1

STEP 3

STEP 6

- 150g frozen chopped leaf spinach, thawed, chopped
- 500g fresh ricotta
- 25g finely grated parmesan
- 1 free-range egg
- 2 Tbsp basil pesto, plus extra 2 Tbsp to serve
- Sea-salt flakes and freshly ground black pepper, to season
- 16 dried instant cannelloni tubes
- 700g tomato-based pasta sauce
- ½ cup grated mozzarella
- Basil leaves, to garnish

STEP 1 Squeeze excess moisture from spinach, removing as much liquid as possible. Transfer to a large bowl.

STEP 2 Add ricotta, parmesan, egg and pesto. Stir until well combined. Season and stir again.

STEP 3 Spoon ricotta mixture into a piping bag or large snap-lock bag and snip tip to about 1cm wide. Pipe ricotta mixture into cannelloni tubes to fill.

STEP 4 Pour ½ cup of the pasta sauce into the bowl of a 5L slow cooker and spread to coat base. Pour in 60ml water.

STEP 5 Arrange cannelloni tubes on top of sauce, trying to keep them in a single layer as much as possible.

STEP 6 Pour remaining pasta sauce over cannelloni to cover. Add 500ml water to pasta sauce jar, shake well and pour over top of cannelloni.

STEP 7 Place bowl in appliance, cover with lid and cook on low setting for 2½ hours.

STEP 8 Scatter mozzarella over top of cannelloni. Cover with lid and cook for a further 20 minutes. Remove bowl from appliance and remove lid. To serve, top with extra pesto and basil.

Slow-cooked tomato Napoletana sauce
Recipe, see page 140

SLOW-COOKED TOMATO NAPOLETANA SAUCE

A quality homemade sauce is the secret to absolutely mouth-watering tomato-based Italian meals. This is good enough to impress Nonna, the toughest of all critics!

METHOD SLOW COOKER **PREP** 10 MINS **COOK** 6 HOURS **MAKES** 7 CUPS

2 x 800g cans diced tomatoes
¼ cup tomato paste
¼ cup extra virgin olive oil
1 brown onion, finely chopped
2 cloves garlic, crushed
1 cup basil leaves
Sea-salt flakes and freshly ground black pepper, to season

STEP 1 Put tomatoes, tomato paste, olive oil, onion and garlic in the bowl of a 5L slow cooker. Stir in ½ of the basil. Place bowl in appliance, cover with lid and cook on low setting for 6 hours.

STEP 2 Remove bowl from appliance and remove lid. Season, stir in remaining basil and use.

SERVING SUGGESTION

PAPPARDELLE NAPOLETANA To make, cook 400g dried pappardelle in a large saucepan of boiling salted water following packet instructions. Drain, reserving 125ml hot pasta water. Meanwhile, heat 4 cups cooked Napoletana sauce in a large saucepan over a medium heat. Add drained pasta and reserved pasta water and toss to combine. Serve topped with torn bocconcini balls and basil leaves. Serves 4.

COOK'S TIPS

• To store, pour hot sauce into sterilised jars (see glossary, page 184) and seal. Store in the fridge for up to 1 week. Or, cool sauce to room temperature and ladle into labelled snap-lock bags. Seal, expelling air. Freeze flat. Sauce will keep in the freezer for up to 3 months.
• To thaw, put bag in a large bowl and leave in fridge overnight, then reheat in the microwave or a large saucepan until hot.

FRESH-BAKED HERB BREAD

You can cook bread in the slow cooker. Really! And you know what? It's all kinds of amazing. Plus, there's no kneading required. This loaf is best eaten on the day of cooking.

METHOD SLOW COOKER **PREP** 10 MINS PLUS 2 HOURS PROVING **COOK** 2 HOURS 15 MINS **SERVES** 6-8

- 7g sachet (2 tsp) instant dry yeast
- 2 tsp sea-salt flakes, plus extra 1 tsp
- 1 Tbsp extra virgin olive oil, plus extra to serve
- 3½ cups plain flour
- 2 tsp dried Italian herb mix, plus extra ½ tsp
- 6 small sprigs rosemary

STEP 1 Put yeast, salt, oil and 400ml lukewarm water in a large bowl.

STEP 2 Stir with a wooden spoon.

STEP 3 Add flour and herb mix, then stir until a wet dough comes together.

STEP 4 Cover with plastic wrap and set aside at room temperature for 2 hours to prove (rise).

STEP 5 Line base and at least halfway up the side of the bowl of a 5L slow cooker with a sheet of baking paper.

STEP 6 Using damp hands, pick up dough and transfer to prepared slow cooker bowl, pushing it down with fingertips to flatten until it covers most of the base.

STEP 7 Scatter top of dough with extra salt and extra herb mix. Push sprigs of rosemary into dough.

STEP 8 Place bowl in appliance, cover with a piece of paper towel, cover with lid and cook on high setting for 2 hours 15 minutes. Remove bowl from appliance and remove lid.

STEP 9 Remove bread from appliance. Serve as is or, for a golden crust, preheat oven grill to high. Cook bread under grill for 1-2 minutes, or until golden, watching closely to ensure bread doesn't burn. Serve with extra oil.

COOK'S TIP

For an extra dose of flavour, you could pair your bread with homemade herb butter. Simply soften some unsalted butter to room temperature and mix in freshly chopped herbs or grated lemon zest to taste. Form into a log, wrap in plastic wrap and chill until firm.

CREAMY MASHED POTATO

A great all-rounder, sebago potatoes are readily available at the supermarket.

METHOD STOVE TOP **PREP** 10 MINS **COOK** 25 MINS **SERVES** 4-6 AS A SIDE DISH

- 1.2kg sebago potatoes, washed, peeled, cut into large chunks
- 3 tsp fine sea-salt flakes, plus extra to season
- 100g unsalted butter, chopped
- 125ml thickened cream
- Freshly ground black pepper, to season

COOK'S TIPS

- Want to make your mash healthier? Use milk instead of cream and omit the butter.
- Potatoes provide a good amount of vitamin C and fibre. However, the fibre benefits are far greater when the skins are left on. So, if you need more fibre in your diet, cook and mash them skin and all. It saves on peeling, too!

STEP 1 Put potato chunks in a large saucepan with fine salt and cover with cold water. Bring to the boil over a high heat, then reduce to medium. Simmer for 20 minutes, or until tender.

STEP 2 Drain potato and return to pan.

STEP 3 For a chunky-style result, squish potato chunks with a masher.

STEP 4 If you prefer smoother mash, push them through a ricer or sieve.

STEP 5 Put butter and cream in a small saucepan over a medium heat and bring to a simmer. Cook for 2 minutes, or until butter has melted. Season.

STEP 6 Remove from heat and add to warm mashed potato.

STEP 7 Beat with a wooden spoon until well combined. Serve.

FLAVOURED MASHED POTATOES

Transform your basic mashed potato into a creamy, show-stopping side.

METHOD STOVE TOP **PREP** 25 MINS **COOK** 25 MINS **SERVES** 4-6 AS A SIDE DISH

1 quantity Creamy mashed potato (see recipe, page 144), adding in the combinations below as per instructions

PINE NUTS AND PESTO

2 Tbsp basil pesto sauce

1 Tbsp pine nuts

CHEESE AND GARLIC

1 clove garlic, finely grated

⅓ cup finely grated parmesan

1 Tbsp mascarpone

MUSTARD

2 tsp Dijon mustard OR

2 tsp wholegrain mustard

(for a strong mustard flavour, try adding a little extra after tasting)

PARSLEY AND LEMON

2 Tbsp finely chopped parsley

1 tsp finely grated lemon zest

PINE NUTS AND PESTO

Swirl through basil pesto and pine nuts in Step 7.

TRY THIS Italian combo with chicken or pork.

CHEESE AND GARLIC

Add grated garlic in Step 5. Then, stir in grated parmesan and mascarpone in Step 7.

TRY THIS Rich and hearty, serve with slow-cooked red meat.

MUSTARD

Add Dijon or wholegrain mustard in Step 7.

TRY THIS Pair with beef for an added punchy bite.

PARSLEY AND LEMON

Fold in chopped parsley and grated lemon zest in Step 7.

TRY THIS This light, zesty mix matches well with seafood.

HOW TO MAKE
BETTER MASH

- First, choose the right potato. Use a starchy variety or an all-rounder such as sebago (as used for our mash), desiree, pontiac or golden delight. Avoid waxy potatoes.
- When boiling, start with cold water to ensure potatoes cook evenly and entirely at a slow, steady pace.
- Salt the water to give potatoes flavour as they cook.
- Heat butter and cream before adding as they're harder to incorporate when cold. They also cool down hot mash.
- Don't overbeat your mash – you'll get a sticky mess more like glue than a fluffy side.

HOMEMADE EGG PASTA

All you need is flour, an egg and a pinch of salt. It's really that easy!

PREP 25 MINS PLUS SETTING/CHILLING   **COOK** NIL   **SERVES** 1

100g plain flour, plus extra to dust
Pinch fine sea-salt flakes
1 free-range egg

COOK'S TIPS

- For best results, use eggs at room temperature. If your eggs have been chilled, put them in a bowl of warm water for a few minutes before use.
- If chilling the pasta dough overnight, remove from fridge 30 minutes before using.
- Fresh pasta is best cooked on the same day. It doesn't need a long cooking time, generally between 1½-2 minutes in salted, boiling water.

STEP 1 Dust a clean, dry surface with extra flour. Mound flour on surface and add salt. Make a well in the centre wide enough to contain the egg.

STEP 2 Crack egg into a cup, then pour into well. Whisk egg with a fork until lightly beaten. Use fork to swirl egg, then continue to swirl egg, adding in a little flour, swirling and adding more flour until all flour has been incorporated and a very rough, loose mixture forms. Use your hands to bring the dough together, forming a rough, sticky dough.

STEP 3 Use the heel of your hand to knead dough, pushing dough down and forward, then turning dough clockwise 45° and continuing with pushing and turning for at least 5 minutes, or until a smooth, soft, silky dough forms. If dough is too sticky, gradually add small amounts of flour, a sprinkle at a time. If too dry, add a very small amount of cold water, 1 teaspoon at a time.

STEP 4 Form dough into a flat disc and wrap in plastic wrap. Set aside for 30-60 minutes. You can chill overnight if more convenient.

STEP 5 Cut dough into quarters. Put one quarter on the bench and rewrap remaining dough in plastic wrap.

STEP 6 Form quarter of dough into a rough rectangle using your hands.

STEP 7 Pass dough rectangle through a pasta machine at the thickest setting. Continue to pass dough through the machine, folding it in half each time, reducing the setting after every 3 passes through the machine, lightly dusting dough with a little flour as necessary. If pasta gets too long and difficult to work with, cut sheet into smaller, more workable-sized pieces.

STEP 8 Repeat with the remaining dough quarters. At this point you can make sheets, fettuccine, tagliatelle or other pasta shapes of your choice.

STEP 9 Once you have cut the pasta into desired shapes, dust with a little flour to ensure it doesn't stick together, then it's ready to cook (see Cook's tips, above left).

MULLED WINE

Smooth and silky, with a delicious hint of chilly nights, you'll never make an easier or more impressive batch drink than mulled wine. Just pour, set and relax!

METHOD SLOW COOKER   **PREP** 5 MINS   **COOK** 1 HOUR   **SERVES** 4-6

1 orange
1 lemon
750ml bottle chianti
¼ cup brown sugar
2 tsp vanilla bean paste
2 sticks cinnamon
2 star anise

STEP 1 Peel strips of zest from orange and lemon using a vegetable peeler.

STEP 2 Put zest in the bowl of a 5.7L slow cooker. Add remaining ingredients.

STEP 3 Cover with lid.

STEP 4 Cook on the low setting for 1 hour. Turn setting to keep warm and serve with a ladle, allowing your guests to help themselves.

COOK'S TIP

If you have orange liqueur sitting in your pantry, you can add 40ml when adding the wine.

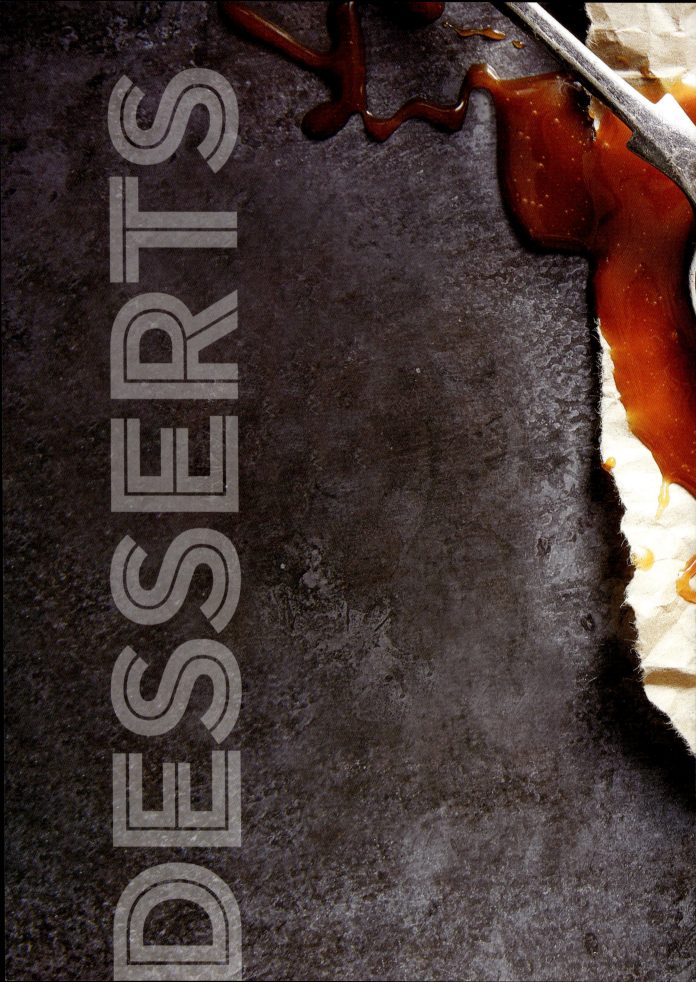
DESSERTS

SELF-SAUCING STICKY DATE AND BANANA PUDDING

Transform ripe banana into a warming pud. Sticky date is always a hit with everyone!

METHOD SLOW COOKER **PREP** 15 MINS PLUS 40 MINS SOFTENING/STANDING **COOK** 2 HOURS 15 MINS **SERVES** 6

150g pitted dates, roughly chopped

½ tsp bicarbonate of soda

½ cup milk

1 free-range egg

50g unsalted butter, melted, plus extra 50g chopped

1 tsp vanilla bean paste

2 cups brown sugar

1½ cups self-raising flour

1 tsp mixed spice

1 ripe banana, mashed

Cocoa powder, to dust

Double cream, to serve

Walnuts, roughly chopped, to serve

STEP 1 Put dates and bicarbonate of soda in a small bowl. Pour over ½ cup of boiling water and set aside for 30 minutes to soften.

STEP 2 Put milk, egg, melted butter and vanilla in a large jug. Whisk to combine, then whisk in ½ of the sugar. Sift flour and spice into a large bowl. Make a well in centre, then pour in milk mixture. Whisk until smooth. Mash date mixture with a fork, then stir into batter, along with banana. Pour batter into the bowl of a 5L slow cooker.

STEP 3 Sprinkle remaining sugar over the top, then scatter over extra chopped butter. Gently pour over 3 cups of boiling water. Place bowl in appliance and cover with lid. Cook on high setting for 2 hours 15 minutes, or until cake is firm. Remove lid and stand for 10 minutes before dusting with cocoa. Serve with cream and walnuts.

APPLE BERRY CRUMBLE

Everyone needs a brilliant crumble in their bag of tricks! It's a crowd-pleasing dessert, and you can even eat the leftovers as an indulgent brekkie granola!

METHOD OVEN **PREP** 10 MINS PLUS COOLING **COOK** 1 HOUR **SERVES** 4

- 4 Granny Smith apples (about 800g in total), peeled, cored
- 2 cups frozen mixed berries
- ⅓ cup caster sugar
- Cream, custard or ice-cream, to serve

CRUMBLE TOPPING
- 1 cup plain flour
- 120g unsalted butter, chilled, chopped
- ½ cup brown sugar
- ½ cup rolled oats
- 1 tsp ground cinnamon

STEP 1 Preheat oven to 160°C fan-forced (180°C conventional). Cut apples into 2cm cubes and put in a small roasting pan or slice tin (about 30 x 20cm). Add berries and sugar and toss to combine, then cover with foil. Put pan in a larger oven tray to catch any cooking juices. Bake for 20 minutes.

STEP 2 Meanwhile, to make crumble topping, put flour in a large bowl. Add butter, rubbing together with fingers until it resembles coarse breadcrumbs. Add remaining topping ingredients and rub together.

STEP 3 Remove pan from oven and discard foil. Spread topping evenly over fruit to cover. Bake for a further 35 minutes, or until topping is golden and fruit is bubbling.

STEP 4 Allow to cool for 5 minutes. Serve crumble warm with cream, custard or ice-cream.

COOK'S TIP

To increase the sweetness of this dish, crumble some of your favourite plain biscuits, such as gingernuts, in the topping.

SLOW-COOKED ROSÉ RHUBARB

Stewed in sugar and rosé wine, tangy rhubarb becomes a delectable winter warmer for dessert lovers.

METHOD OVEN **PREP** 5 MINS **COOK** 1 HOUR 20 MINS **SERVES** 6

- 1 large bunch rhubarb, leaves discarded, stalks trimmed (about 500g)
- 1 cup caster sugar
- 60ml rosé wine
- Thickened cream, to drizzle
- Caramel macadamias (see recipe, below right), to sprinkle

STEP 1 Preheat oven to 120°C fan-forced (140°C conventional). Slice rhubarb into lengths to fit snugly in a 25 x 20cm roasting pan. Add sugar, tossing well to coat, then arrange rhubarb in a single layer. Pour over wine.

STEP 2 Cover pan tightly with foil to ensure steam doesn't escape. Bake for 1 hour 20 minutes, or until rhubarb is very tender and a sweet, sticky sauce has formed.

STEP 3 Serve drizzled with cream and sprinkled with caramel macadamias.

HOW TO MAKE
CARAMEL MACADAMIAS

Put ½ cup roughly chopped macadamias, 2 Tablespoons brown sugar and 15g chopped unsalted butter in a large frying pan over a high heat. Cook, stirring, for 3 minutes, or until nuts are golden and sugar is caramelised. Pour onto a baking paper-lined oven tray and set aside for 10 minutes, or until cool and firm. Break into bite-sized pieces.

ROSÉ RHUBARB SPONGE PUDDINGS

Want to up the presentation value of your rosé rhubarb?
Make a simple batter, dollop on top and bake. Yum!

METHOD OVEN   **PREP** 5 MINS   **COOK** 15 MINS   **SERVES** 6

60g unsalted butter, melted

1 free-range egg

½ cup caster sugar

1 tsp vanilla extract

Finely grated zest of 1 orange

¼ cup milk

1 cup plain flour

1 tsp baking powder

1 quantity Slow-cooked rosé rhubarb (see recipe, page 158), ideally hot (see Cook's tips, right)

Double cream, to serve

Caramel macadamias (see recipe, page 158), to serve

STEP 1 Preheat oven to 180°C fan-forced (200°C conventional). Put butter, egg, sugar, vanilla and zest in a large bowl. Using an electric hand mixer, beat for 2 minutes. Add milk, then sift in flour and baking powder. Beat again until light and fluffy.

STEP 2 Divide Slow-cooked rosé rhubarb between six 1-cup capacity ovenproof dishes (see Cook's tips, below) and dollop batter on each. Bake for 15 minutes, or until golden brown. Serve with double cream and caramel macadamias.

COOK'S TIPS

- If you're using cold leftover cooked rhubarb, bake puddings for an extra 5 minutes to ensure they're hot.
- You can also make this pudding in the same dish in which you baked the Slow-cooked rosé rhubarb. Just dollop spoonfuls of batter evenly on top of rhubarb. The batter will join together as it cooks.

SIMPLE CHOCOLATE CAKE

Who knew you could whip up this afternoon tea staple without an oven – or even a tray? Once you've seen how simple it is, you'll never look back.

METHOD SLOW COOKER **PREP** 10 MINS PLUS COOLING **COOK** 2 HOURS **SERVES** 8-10

Melted unsalted butter, to grease, plus extra 60g melted

1 cup self-raising flour

⅓ cup cocoa powder

¾ cup caster sugar

125ml milk

2 free-range eggs, lightly beaten

1 tsp vanilla extract

Double cream, to serve

Fresh berries, to serve

Chocolate topping, to serve

STEP 1 Grease the bowl of a 5L slow cooker and line with a large sheet of baking paper to cover the base and 3cm up the side.

STEP 2 Sift flour and cocoa into a large bowl, then stir in sugar.

STEP 3 Make a well in the centre and pour in milk, eggs, vanilla and extra melted butter.

STEP 4 Use a whisk to beat until a smooth batter forms. Pour into prepared bowl.

STEP 5 Place bowl in appliance. Cover with lid and cook on the high setting for 2 hours.

STEP 6 Remove bowl from appliance, remove lid and remove cake from the bowl. Set aside to cool for 30 minutes.

STEP 7 Serve cake with double cream, fresh berries and chocolate topping.

OVERNIGHT PORRIDGE

Feeding a crowd? Put this porridge on to cook just before you go to sleep and wake up to brekkie done.

METHOD SLOW COOKER **PREP** 10 MINS **COOK** 8 HOURS **SERVES** 8

- 2 cups wholegrain steel-cut oats
- 1 tsp ground cinnamon
- 1L milk
- 1L water
- 2 apples, unpeeled, cored, roughly chopped
- Brown sugar, nuts, yoghurt and fresh fruit, to serve

STEP 1 Put all ingredients in the bowl of a 5L slow cooker.

STEP 2 Stir to roughly mix together, then place bowl in appliance. Cover with lid and cook on the low setting for 8 hours.

STEP 3 Remove bowl from appliance and remove lid. Serve with sugar, nuts, yoghurt and fresh fruit.

COOK'S TIPS

- Any leftover porridge can be reheated the next day in the microwave, adding a little milk to help loosen the oats.
- Steel-cut oats are available from health food stores and the health food aisle of large supermarkets. Do not use quick oats or plain wholegrain rolled oats for this recipe.

LEMONADE SCONES

The crunchy base and fluffy centre of these teatime treats will make you love your slow cooker even more than you already do.

METHOD SLOW COOKER   **PREP** 15 MINS   **COOK** 1 HOUR   **MAKES** 9

3 cups self-raising flour
250ml thickened cream
250ml lemonade, at room temperature
Icing sugar mixture, to dust
Jam and whipped cream, to serve

STEP 1 Grease the bowl of a 5.7L slow cooker appliance and line with a large sheet of baking paper to cover the base and 3cm up the side.

STEP 2 Put flour in a large bowl. Combine cream and lemonade in a jug and pour into the centre of the flour. Use a butter knife to combine, using a cutting action to bring the dough together. Turn out onto a lightly floured surface and shape into a 3cm-high oval. Use a 7cm round cookie cutter to cut out 9 scones.

STEP 3 Arrange scones in prepared appliance bowl. Cover the opening of the appliance bowl with a tea towel, ensuring the towel doesn't touch the scone dough, then cover with lid. Fold up the tea towel edges so they cover the outside of the lid. Cook on the high setting for 1 hour.

STEP 4 Remove bowl from appliance, remove lid and tea towel, then remove scones. Dust scones with icing sugar mixture, then serve with jam and cream.

COOK'S TIP

Strawberry jam is a classic, but any sort of fruit jam or conserve will pair beautifully with these scones and cream. Think apricot, blackcurrant or even a dab of lemon curd.

ITALIAN CITRUS, OLIVE OIL AND POLENTA PUDDING

Combine oranges and lemons with polenta to create a divine dessert.

METHOD SLOW COOKER **PREP** 10 MINS **COOK** 2 HOURS **SERVES** 8

- 1 cup self-raising flour, sifted
- ½ cup fine polenta
- 2 cups caster sugar
- 200ml milk
- 120ml light-flavoured extra virgin olive oil
- 1 free-range egg
- Finely grated zest and juice of 2 lemons (100ml juice needed)
- Finely grated zest and juice of 1 orange (100ml juice needed)
- Icing sugar mixture, to dust
- Toasted flaked almonds, sliced orange rounds, double cream and micro basil leaves, to top

STEP 1 Combine flour, polenta and 1 cup of the caster sugar in a large bowl. Make a well in the centre and add milk, oil, egg and zests. Whisk to form a smooth batter.

STEP 2 Pour batter into the bowl of a 5L slow cooker and place in appliance.

STEP 3 Combine juices, remaining caster sugar and 350ml boiling water. Pour mixture over the back of a large spoon directly onto batter. Cover with lid and cook on the high setting for 2 hours.

STEP 4 Remove bowl from appliance and remove lid. Divide pudding between bowls, dust with icing sugar and top with almonds, orange slices, cream and basil to serve.

COOK'S TIP

Serve this dessert topped with chocolate curls for a luxe, jaffa-flavoured pudding.

CHOCOLATE TIRAMISU SELF-SAUCING PUDDING

All the tiramisu flavours you love are encapsulated in this decadent chocolate pud, spiked with liqueur of course!

METHOD SLOW COOKER **PREP** 15 MINS **COOK** 2 HOURS **SERVES** 6

- 100g unsalted butter, melted, plus extra to grease
- 200ml milk
- 1 free-range egg
- 1 cup caster sugar
- 1½ cups self-raising flour
- 5 Tbsp cocoa powder, sifted, plus extra to serve
- 10 savoiardi (Italian sponge biscuits), roughly chopped, plus extra to serve
- ¼ cup dark chocolate bits
- 1 cup brown sugar
- 400ml hot black coffee
- 2 Tbsp Kahlua or Tia Maria (coffee-flavoured liqueur)
- Mascarpone, to dollop
- Thickened cream, to drizzle

STEP 1 Grease the bowl of a 5L slow cooker.

STEP 2 Put 100g melted butter, milk and egg in a large bowl. Whisk until smooth.

STEP 3 Add caster sugar and whisk again until combined. Sift in flour and 2 Tablespoons of the cocoa, then whisk until combined.

STEP 4 Spoon batter into prepared slow cooker bowl. Arrange chopped biscuits on top and scatter with chocolate bits.

STEP 5 Put brown sugar and remaining cocoa in a large jug or bowl. Stir in hot coffee, liqueur and 150ml boiling water.

STEP 6 Pour brown sugar mixture over the back of a large spoon directly onto batter. Place bowl in appliance, cover with lid and cook on the high setting for 2 hours, or until cake is firm and sauce forms underneath.

STEP 7 Remove bowl from appliance and remove lid. Divide pudding between serving bowls. Dollop with mascarpone and drizzle over cream. Serve with extra biscuits to dip into the sauce.

BUTTERSCOTCH PUDDINGS WITH ESPRESSO CARAMEL SAUCE

Give a classic pud a tasty twist with coffee-flavoured caramel sauce. Don't forget the cream. Delish!

METHOD OVEN **PREP** 25 MINS **COOK** 25 MINS **SERVES** 4

Cooking oil spray, to grease
100g unsalted butter, melted
⅓ cup dark brown sugar
1 free-range egg, lightly beaten
80ml milk
⅓ cup golden syrup
1⅓ cups self-raising flour
Double cream, to serve

ESPRESSO CARAMEL SAUCE
½ cup caster sugar
60ml water
60ml thickened cream
60ml hot black espresso coffee

STEP 1 Preheat oven to 180°C fan-forced (200°C conventional). Grease 4 shallow 3-cup capacity ovenproof bowls with cooking oil spray and transfer to a large oven tray. Combine melted butter and brown sugar in a large bowl. Add the egg, milk and golden syrup and stir until combined. Sift in flour and stir until a smooth batter forms.

STEP 2 Spoon mixture evenly into bowls. Bake for 25 minutes, or until a skewer inserted into the centre comes out clean.

STEP 3 Meanwhile, to make espresso caramel sauce, combine sugar and water in a medium saucepan over a low heat. Cook, stirring, until sugar has dissolved. Bring to the boil. Boil, without stirring, for 10 minutes, or until mixture becomes golden, brushing down side of pan with cold water if sugar crystals start to form. Remove from heat and stir in thickened cream and espresso coffee. Return to the heat, reduce heat to low and cook, stirring, for 2 minutes, or until sauce has thickened and is smooth. Set aside to cool for 10 minutes.

STEP 4 Spoon cream on top of puddings and drizzle generously with espresso caramel sauce to serve.

COOK'S TIP

Not a coffee drinker? For an easy switch out, top pudding with double cream and store-bought caramel topping instead of espresso caramel sauce.

THE BEST CUTS

The best pieces of meat for slow cooking are those considered 'secondary cuts'. These contain more connective tissue, which needs a long, slow cook to help break down the tough bits. The result? A super-tender, fall-apart meal. Plus, they're cheaper, so leave the expensive, lean cuts for quick-to-cook recipes.

1. PORK AND BEEF MINCE are popular choices for feeding the kids. Mince breaks up into small pieces, so it's easy for them to eat.

2. BEEF CHUCK STEAK is cut from the neck and shoulder. It's affordable and readily available diced. If you're planning to cook a whole piece, it's best to order it from your butcher a day in advance.

3. PORK SHOULDER is sold as large portions, with or without the bone. You can use diced shoulder, too – it allows the meat to fit easily into a saucepan or slow cooker. If you do use it diced, remove the fat.

4. LAMB SHANKS are cut from the leg. You can either buy forequarter shanks, which are smaller as they're from the front legs, or the larger hindquarter shanks, which are taken from the back legs. The shanks pictured here are not 'Frenched', which is the most common way to buy them. French trimming is when a portion of the bone has been scraped clean, removing the gristle and meat. You can use Frenched shanks if you prefer, but you get less meat for your money and the bone is often exposed after cooking anyway.

5. CHICKEN THIGH FILLETS AND CUTLETS are affordable and readily available. Use skinless pieces to reduce the fat content.

6. GRAVY BEEF, also known as beef shin, comes from the cow's lower shin and looks quite marbly. It's similar to osso buco, but osso buco contains the shin bone.

7. BEEF SHORT RIBS are incredibly meaty and have a layer of fat on top. Cook them with the fat on, or remove this prior to cooking. Order ribs from your butcher a day in advance as they're not readily available at the supermarket.

HEALTHY OPTIONS

Add these fresh ingredients to your cooking repertoire to ensure the whole family consumes a wide range of nutrients and antioxidants, such as vitamins A, B, C and E; minerals such as zinc, magnesium and potassium; and prebiotics and probiotics. All of these will help your body protect itself from colds, flus and other ailments.

---

1. GREEK-STYLE YOGHURT contains probiotics (healthy bacteria), which keep the gut free from disease-causing germs.

2. APPLE CIDER VINEGAR aids gut health and wards off colds. Choose one with a 'mother' culture.

3. RED MEAT AND CHICKEN are a good source of zinc. The protein also helps the body recover from illness.

4. EXTRA VIRGIN OLIVE OIL supports the absorption of the antioxidant carotenoid.

5. PULSES contain prebiotics (indigestible food fibres), which help probiotics do their job.

6. TOMATO (fresh and canned) is rich in cell-protecting lycopene.

7. ORANGES AND LEMONS contain vitamin C, which helps the body defend against bacterial infections.

8. CARROTS contain antioxidants that fight infection and support a healthy gut lining.

9. RED CAPSICUM provides vitamins A and C.

10. BABY SPINACH contains carotenoids, vitamins, iron and protein.

11. RED CABBAGE has antiviral and antibacterial agents and vitamin C.

12. WATERCRESS is a great source of vitamins A, C and K.

13. ONION can help break down mucus, thanks to the nutrient quercetin.

14. SWEET POTATO has carotenoids.

15. CHILLI is a wonderful source of vitamin C. Plus, the hotties can make you sweat, increasing activity in the immune system.

16. TURMERIC, a natural antibiotic, contains potassium and manganese, which support healthy immune function.

17. GINGER can kill cold-causing bacteria, is an anti-inflammatory and contains antibiotics. It can soothe the throat and reduce a fever.

18. GARLIC is a natural antibiotic.

HOW TO MAKE LEFTOVERS SOUP

Sometimes the best meals don't follow a recipe and can't be written down. All you need is a few leftovers, a little inspiration and a clever eye in the pantry

1 Use up leftover meat and veg
Add ingredients such as roasted or steamed vegetables, roasted meat or chicken and even bones such as lamb shanks with the meat removed. Just make sure all leftovers have been handled with care and promptly refrigerated to maintain food safety.

2 Search the pantry for substance
TRY
- Two-minute noodles
- Dried or canned chickpeas, lentils, peas and beans
- Rice and pasta
- Canned vegetables such as tomatoes, corn and peas
- Potatoes and onions

3 Add flavour
TRY
- Garlic
- Pizza sauce
- Vegemite
- Pitted olives and other antipasto vegetables
- Peanut butter
- Pesto
- Mustard
- Sweet chilli sauce
- Salsa
- Dried herbs
- Curry paste
- Honey
- Wine

4 Add stock or water to cover your ingredients
Use chicken, beef or vegetable stock in liquid, powder or cubed form.

5 Cook and eat!
Put all your ingredients in a pot and let it simmer on the stove for anywhere from 20 minutes to 2 hours, or until ingredients are tender and your soup is scrumptious. Serve and enjoy!

SOUP TOPPERS

Sprinkle your creation with crunchy, tasty bits! These provide an extra flavour hit and another dimension of texture. Pick one or many!

SOUPER-EASY

No effort needed, straight from the packet.

- Corn chips
- Mini pappadums
- Crispy fried noodles
- Chopped nuts, such as roasted almonds
- Basil pesto
- Mascarpone, sour cream or Greek-style yoghurt

SOUP IT UP

A bit of effort, a lot of flavour.

- Pan-fried store-bought dumplings – great for Asian-style soups
- Crispy prosciutto or bacon bits (see instructions, above right)

ON THE SIDE

- Grilled cheese melts or toasties
- Avo toasts (see recipe, page 26)

TO MAKE crispy prosciutto, line an oven tray with baking paper. Preheat oven to 180°C fan-forced (200°C conventional). Arrange 4 thin slices of prosciutto in a single layer on prepared tray. Top with a second sheet of baking paper and a second tray to gently squash prosciutto. Bake for 10 minutes, or until golden. Remove second tray and second sheet of baking paper and bake for a further 3–5 minutes, or until browned. To serve, slice in half on the diagonal.

TO MAKE crispy bacon bits, keep the oven at the same temperature. Line an oven tray with baking paper. Finely chop 2 rashers of rindless middle bacon and arrange on prepared tray. Bake, stirring halfway through, for 10 minutes, or until golden and crispy. Set aside for 5 minutes to cool then serve.

GLOSSARY

agrodolce sweet and sour sauce flavoured with vinegar, sugar and red onion.
anchovies small oily fish. Anchovy fillets are preserved and packed in oil or salt in small cans or jars, and are strong in flavour. Fresh anchovies are much milder.
baby kale the younger, smaller leaves of kale, often likely to be more tender and mild in flavour than larger kale leaves.
baby spinach best eaten raw in salads; the larger leaves should be added last to soups, stews and stir-fries, and should be cooked until barely wilted.
baking powder a raising agent consisting mainly of 2 parts cream of tartar to 1 part bicarbonate of soda.
barley nutritious grain used in soups and stews. Hulled barley, the least processed, is high in fibre. Pearl barley has had the husk removed, then been steamed and polished so only the 'pearl' of the original grain remains, much the same as white rice.
basil sweet basil is the most common type of basil, used extensively in Italian dishes, and is one of the main ingredients in pesto.
basil pesto flavourful sauce made with basil, pine nuts, garlic, olive oil and parmesan.
bay leaves aromatic leaves from the bay tree, available fresh or dried; they have a strong, slightly peppery flavour.
beans
borlotti also called Roman beans or pink beans; can be eaten fresh or dried. Interchangeable with pinto beans due to their similarity in appearance.
butter large beige beans with a mealy texture and mild taste. Cans labelled butter beans are, in fact, cannellini beans. Confusingly, butter bean is also another name for lima bean.
cannellini small white beans similar in appearance and flavour to other white beans (great northern, navy or haricot), all of which can be substituted for the other. Available dried or canned.
green also known as French or string beans, these long, thin fresh beans are consumed in their entirety once cooked.
kidney medium-sized red beans, slightly floury in texture yet sweet in flavour; sold dried or canned.
bicarbonate of soda also known as baking soda; a leavening agent.
broccolini cross between broccoli and Chinese kale, it has long, asparagus-like stems with a long loose floret; both are edible. Resembles broccoli but is milder and sweeter.
butternut pumpkin can sometimes be known as butternut squash; offers a sweet and nutty flavour.
capers the grey-green buds of a warm climate (usually Mediterranean) shrub, sold either dried and salted or pickled in a vinegar brine. Tiny young ones, called baby capers, are also available both in brine or dried in salt.
capsicum also called bell pepper; comes in many colours including red, green, yellow, orange and purplish-black. Discard seeds and membrane before use.
caramelised onion relish a delicious accompaniment to cold meats, it has a real sweet and savoury flavour from slowly cooking the onions to release their natural sweetness.
cheese
bocconcini walnut-sized, baby mozzarella; a delicate, semi-soft white cheese traditionally made from buffalo milk. Sold fresh, it spoils rapidly so will only keep, refrigerated in brine, for 1 or 2 days at the most.
feta Greek in origin; a crumbly-textured goat's or sheep's milk cheese boasting a sharp, salty taste. Ripened and stored in salted whey.
mascarpone Italian fresh cultured cream product made in much the same way as yoghurt. Whiteish to creamy yellow in colour, with a soft, creamy, buttery-rich, luscious texture.
mozzarella soft, spun-curd cheese, originating in southern Italy, where it was traditionally made from water buffalo milk. Now generally made from cow's milk, it is the most popular pizza cheese for its low melting point and elasticity when heated.
parmesan also called parmigiano; a hard, grainy, cow's milk cheese originating in the Parma region of Italy.
ricotta a soft, sweet, moist, white cow's milk cheese with a low fat content (8.5%) and a slightly grainy texture. The name roughly translates as 'cooked again' and refers to ricotta's manufacture from a whey that is itself a by-product of other cheese-making.
chianti style of red wine made primarily with sangiovese grapes from the Tuscany region of Italy
chicken maryland chicken cut where the leg and thigh are still connected in a single piece; bones and skin intact.
chickpeas (garbanzo beans) also called hummus or channa; irregularly round, sandy-coloured legumes used extensively in Mediterranean, Indian and Hispanic cooking. They have a firm texture even after cooking, a floury mouth-feel and nutty flavour; available canned or dried (reconstitute for several hours in cold water before use).
chilli
flakes also sold as crushed chilli; dehydrated, deep-red, extremely fine slices and whole seeds.
long red available fresh and dried; a generic term for any moderately hot, long chilli (about 6cm to 8cm long).
chinese five spice a fragrant mixture of ground cinnamon, cloves, star anise, Sichuan pepper and fennel seeds. Used in Chinese and other Asian cooking; available from most supermarkets or Asian food shops.
chives (fresh) related to the onion and leek; has a subtle onion flavour. Used more for flavour than as an ingredient; chopped finely, it's good in sauces, dressings, omelettes or as a garnish.
chorizo sausage of Spanish origin, made from coarsely ground pork and highly seasoned with garlic and chilli. It is deeply smoked, very spicy and dry-cured, so does not need cooking.
cinnamon available both in the piece (called sticks or quills) and ground into powder; one of the world's most common spices, used universally as a sweet, fragrant flavouring for both sweet and savoury foods.
cocoa powder also known as unsweetened cocoa; cocoa beans (cacao seeds) that have been fermented, roasted, shelled, ground into powder then cleared of most of the fat content.
coconut
cream obtained commercially from the first pressing of the coconut flesh alone, without the addition of water. Available in cans and cartons at most supermarkets.
milk not the liquid found inside the fruit (coconut water), but the diluted liquid from the second pressing of the white flesh of a mature coconut. Available in cans and cartons at most supermarkets.
coriander a bright-green leafy herb with a pungent flavour. Both stems and roots of coriander are used in cooking; wash well before using. Also available ground or as seeds; these should not be substituted for fresh as the tastes are different.
couscous a fine, grain-like cereal product made from semolina and from the countries of North Africa. A semolina flour and water dough is sieved then dehydrated to produce minuscule, even-sized pellets of couscous; it is rehydrated by steaming, or with the addition of a warm liquid, and swells to

three or four times its size. Eaten like rice or as a salad ingredient.

cream

double (thick) a dolloping cream with a minimum fat content of 45%.

pure also called pouring or fresh cream. It has no additives and contains a minimum fat content of 35%.

thickened (heavy) a whipping cream containing thickener. Minimum fat content 35%.

whipped thickened cream which has been whipped by hand to dolloping consistency.

cumin also known as zeera or comino; resembling caraway in size, cumin is the dried seed of a plant related to the parsley family. It can be purchased either dried as seeds or ground.

curry pastes Some recipes in this book call for commercially prepared pastes of varying strengths and flavours. Use whichever one you feel best suits your spice-level tolerance.

dark (semi-sweet) chocolate also called luxury chocolate; made of a high percentage of cocoa liquor and cocoa butter, and little added sugar.

dutch carrots small, sweet and sold in bunches with the tops still attached.

eschalots also called French or golden shallots, they are small and elongated with a brown skin.

espresso coffee strong coffee brewed by forcing hot water under pressure through darkly roasted, finely ground coffee beans, usually in a machine.

fennel a white to very pale green-white, firm, crisp, roundish vegetable about 8–12cm in diameter. The bulb has a slightly sweet, anise flavour, but the leaves have a much stronger taste.

fennel seeds the name given to the dried seeds of the plant of the same name, which have a stronger licorice flavour.

finger eggplants known as baby or Japanese eggplant; very small and slender so can be used without disgorging.

fish sauce also called nam pla or nuoc nam; made from pulverised salted fermented fish, most often anchovies. It has a very pungent smell and strong taste, so use sparingly or according to your taste level.

flour

plain (all-purpose) unbleached wheat flour, the best for baking: the gluten content ensures a strong dough for a light result.

self-raising all-purpose plain or wholemeal flour with baking powder and salt added; make at home in the proportion of 1 cup plain or wholemeal flour to 2 teaspoons baking powder.

ginger also called green or root ginger; the thick gnarled root of a tropical plant.

gnocchi Italian 'dumplings' made of potatoes, semolina or flour; can be cooked in boiling water or baked with sauce.

golden syrup a by-product of refined sugarcane; pure maple syrup or honey can often be substituted. Treacle is a similar product, however, it is more viscous and has a stronger flavour and aroma than golden syrup (which has been refined further and contains fewer impurities).

granny smith apple with green skin and tart, tough flesh, most commonly used in baking.

greek yoghurt a full-cream yoghurt often made from sheep's milk; its thick, smooth consistency is attained by draining off the milk liquids.

green cabbage a variety of cabbage with smooth and tightly packed leaves, which looks similar in shape to a soccer ball.

green shallots also called French shallots, eschalots or golden shallots. Small and elongated with a brown skin, they grow in tight clusters like garlic.

icing sugar mixture also known as powdered sugar; granulated sugar crushed together with a small amount of cornflour.

italian herb mix a dried herb mix often consisting of thyme, rosemary, marjoram, basil, oregano and sage.

kaffir lime leaves also known as bai magrood. Aromatic leaves of a citrus tree; two glossy dark green leaves joined end to end, forming a rounded hourglass shape. A strip of fresh lime peel may be substituted for each kaffir lime leaf.

kent pumpkin also known as a Jap pumpkin, the Kent has ribbed, grey-green mottled skin and a nutty, deep yellow flesh.

korma curry paste korma is a mix of mostly heat-free spices; forms the base of a mild, slightly nutty-tasting, slow-cooked curry.

leek a member of the onion family, the leek resembles a green onion but is much larger and more subtle in flavour. Tender baby or pencil leeks are essentially young, slender leeks; available early in the season, they can be cooked and eaten whole like asparagus with minimal cooking. Adult leeks are usually trimmed of most of the green tops then chopped or sliced and cooked as an ingredient in stews, casseroles and soups.

lentils (red, brown, green) dried pulses often identified by, and named after, their colour. Eaten by cultures all over the world, most famously, perhaps, in the dhals of India.

malaysian curry paste available in an array of varieties, including red and green.

mango chutney mixture containing mango, spices, sugar and vinegar.

massaman curry paste has a rich, spicy flavour reminiscent of Middle Eastern cooking; favoured by southern Thai cooks for use in hot and sour stew-like curries and satay sauces.

micro herbs small, immature herbs ideal for decorating as garnish due to their small leaves.

mint, fresh the most commonly used variety of mint is spearmint; it has pointed, bright-green leaves and a fresh flavour.

mint jelly known for pairing with lamb, a sauce made with vinegar, sugar and mint.

mixed spice a classic spice mixture generally containing caraway, allspice, coriander, cumin, nutmeg and ginger, although cinnamon and other spices can also be added. Mixed spice is used with fruit and in cakes.

mushrooms

button small, cultivated white mushrooms with a mild flavour.

dried porcini the richest-flavoured mushrooms, also known as cepes. Expensive, but because they are so strongly flavoured, only a small amount is required for any particular dish.

enoki tiny, long-stemmed, pale mushrooms that grow and are sold in clusters, and can be used that way or separated by slicing off the base. They have a mild fruity flavour and are slightly crisp in texture.

flat large, flat mushrooms with a rich earthy flavour, ideal for filling and barbecuing.

king brown tender yet dense texture. Rich, robust flavour. Remain firm and chewy when cooked.

oyster also known as abalone; grey-white mushrooms shaped like a fan. Prized for their smooth texture and subtle, oyster-like flavour.

portobello mature, fully opened Swiss browns; large, dark brown mushrooms with full-bodied flavour; ideal for filling or barbecuing.

shiitake when fresh are also known as Chinese black, forest or golden oak mushrooms. Large, meaty and, although cultivated, have the earthiness and taste of wild mushrooms.

swiss brown also known as Roman or cremini. Light to dark brown mushrooms with full-bodied flavour; suited for use in casseroles or being stuffed and baked.

mustard

dijon pale brown, distinctively flavoured, fairly mild-tasting French mustard.

wholegrain also known as seeded. A French-style coarse-grain mustard made from crushed mustard seeds and Dijon-style French mustard.

noodles

dried soba thin, pale-brown noodle originally from Japan; made from buckwheat and varying proportions of wheat flour. Available dried and fresh, and in flavoured (for instance, green tea) varieties; eaten in soups, stir-fries and, chilled, on their own.

fried small thin noodles, fried until

crunchy. Often used as crunchy toppings for salads or stirfries.
Thai flat rice also known as rice stick noodles. Made from rice flour and water, available flat and wide or very thin (vermicelli). Must be soaked in boiling water to soften.
nutmeg a strong and pungent spice ground from the dried nut of an evergreen tree native to Indonesia. Usually found ground, but the flavour is more intense from a whole nut; available from spice shops, so it's best to grate your own. Used most often in baking and milk-based desserts but also works nicely in savoury dishes. Found in mixed spice mixtures.
nuts
almonds flat, pointy-tipped nuts having a pitted brown shell enclosing a creamy white kernel covered by a brown skin.
flaked paper-thin slices.
peanuts also called groundnut; not in fact a nut but the pod of a legume. We mainly use raw (unroasted) or unsalted roasted peanuts.
walnuts as well as being a good source of fibre and healthy oils, these nuts contain a range of vitamins, minerals and other beneficial plant components called phytochemicals. Each type of nut has a special make-up and walnuts contain the beneficial omega-3 fatty acids.
oats
rolled flattened oat grain rolled into flakes and traditionally used for porridge.
steel-cut made by cutting whole oat groats into pieces using a steel blade. This makes them thicker and requires a longer cooking time.
oils
extra virgin made from ripened olives, extra virgin and virgin are the first and second press, respectively, of the olives and are therefore considered the best; the 'light' and 'extra light' labels refer to the taste, not fat levels.
olive made from ripened olives. Extra virgin and virgin are the best.
sesame used as a flavouring rather than a cooking oil.
olives
black have a richer and more mellow flavour than the green ones and are softer in texture. Sold either plain or in a piquant marinade.
green are those olives harvested before they're fully ripened and are, as a rule, denser and more bitter than the black variety.
onions
brown and white are interchangeable, with white onions boasting the more pungent flesh.
red also known as Spanish, red Spanish or Bermuda onion; a sweet-flavoured, large, purple-red onion.

shallots also called French or golden shallots or eschalots; small and elongated with a brown skin.
oregano mild-flavoured herb, with a slight lemony aroma, best in tomato-based sauces and Greek-style dishes.
oyster sauce Asian in origin, this thick, richly flavoured brown sauce is made from oysters and their brine, cooked with salt and soy sauce, and thickened with starches. Use as a condiment.
panko breadcrumbs also known as Japanese breadcrumbs. They have a lighter texture than Western-style breadcrumbs. Available from Asian food stores and most supermarkets.
pappadums a very thin circular crisp made from a mixture of flour and water, which is fried in oil.
paprika ground, dried, sweet red capsicum (bell pepper); there are many types of paprika available, including sweet, hot, mild and smoked.
parsley and micro parsley versatile herbs with a fresh, earthy flavour. There are about 30 varieties of curly parsley; the flat-leaf variety (also called continental or Italian parsley) is stronger in flavour and darker in colour. Micro-parsley is simply the young plant with smaller, tender leaves.
pasta
cannelloni cylindrical type of pasta shell generally filled, then covered by a sauce and baked.
dried instant cannelloni tubes these cylindrical pasta shells are usually filled, covered by a sauce and then baked.
fettucine pasta cut into ribbon shape strands.
macaroni tube-shaped pasta.
maccheroni calabresi tubular pasta often paired with rich sauces.
penne small tube-shaped pasta with angled ends.
peppercorns
black dried berry of the black pepper.
pickled green peppercorns preserved in a combination of salt and vinegar.
pink dried berry from a type of rose plant grown in Madagascar, usually sold packed in brine (occasionally found freeze-dried); they possess a distinctive pungently sweet taste.
pine nuts also called pignoli; not a nut but a small, cream-coloured kernel from pine cones. They are best roasted before use to bring out the flavour.
pitted dates fruit of the date palm tree; often eaten fresh or dried, on their own or in dishes. Oval and plump, they are thin skinned with a honey-sweet flavour and sticky texture.
polenta also known as cornmeal; a ground, flour-like cereal made of dried corn (maize) and sold in several different

textures. Also the name of the dish made from it.
pomegranate with arils (seeds) dark-red, leathery-skinned fruit about the size of an orange filled with numerous seeds, each wrapped in an edible lucent-crimson pulp with a unique tangy sweet-sour flavour.
pomegranate molasses not to be confused with pomegranate syrup or grenadine, pomegranate molasses is thicker, browner and more concentrated in flavour. It is tart, sharp, slightly sweet and fruity.
potatoes
chat also known as baby potatoes. Small potatoes, often cooked with their skins on.
desiree good all-rounder potato with a pink-red skin and creamy yellow flesh.
sebago white-skin potato, oval; good fried, mashed and baked.
spudlite a creamy, lower-carb potato.
prosciutto a kind of unsmoked Italian ham; salted, air-cured and aged, it is usually eaten uncooked.
puff pastry a type of pastry with light and flaky layers, which puffs on cooking.
pulses an edible seed that grows in a pod, including beans, lentils and peas.
rice
arborio small, round-grain rice well-suited to absorb a large amount of liquid; the high level of starch makes it especially suitable for risottos for its classic creaminess.
basmati white, fragrant long-grained rice; the grains fluff up when cooked. Wash several times before cooking.
brown retains the high-fibre, nutritious bran coating that's removed from white rice when hulled. It takes longer to cook than white rice and has a chewier texture. Once cooked, the long grains stay separate, while the short grains are soft and stickier.
jasmine long-grain white rice recognised around the world as having a perfumed aromatic quality; moist in texture, it clings together after cooking. Sometimes substituted for basmati rice.
ricotta soft, sweet, moist, white cow-milk cheese with a low fat content and a slightly grainy texture. The name roughly translates as 'cooked again' and refers to ricotta's manufacture from a whey that is itself a by-product of other cheese making.
risotto Italian rice dish made with arborio rice and stock cooked until creamy. Flavoured with vegetables or meats.
rosemary leaves/sprigs/dried pungent herb with long, thin pointy leaves; use large and small sprigs, and the leaves are usually chopped finely.
sage leaves pungent herb with narrow, grey-green leaves; slightly bitter with a slightly musty mint aroma. Refrigerate fresh sage wrapped in a paper towel and sealed in a plastic bag for up to 4 days.

sesame seeds black and white are the most common varieties of this small oval seed; however, there are also red and brown varieties. The seeds are used as an ingredient and as a condiment.

silverbeet (swiss chard) also known, incorrectly, as spinach; has fleshy stalks and large leaves, both of which can be prepared as for spinach.

sour cream thick, commercially-cultured soured cream. It has a minimum fat content of 35%.

sourdough slightly chewy, dense style of bread with a crunchy crust. Made by the fermentation of dough, which gives the slightly sour taste.

split peas variety of yellow or green pea grown specifically for drying. When dried, the peas usually split along a natural seam. Whole and split dried peas are available packaged in supermarkets and in bulk in health food stores.

sriracha medium-hot chilli sauce available from Asian food shops and major supermarkets.

star anise dried, star-shaped pod having an astringent, aniseed flavour; used to flavour stocks and marinades. It is also an essential ingredient in five-spice powder.

sterilising jars it's important the jars be as clean as possible; make sure your hands, the preparation area, tea towels and cloths etc are clean, too. The aim is to finish sterilising the jars and lids at the same time the mixture is ready to be bottled; the hot mixture should be bottled into hot, dry, clean jars. Jars that aren't sterilised properly can cause deterioration of the contents during storage. Always start with cleaned, washed jars and lids, then follow one of these methods:

(1) Put the jars and lids through the hottest cycle of a dishwasher without using any detergent.

(2) Lie the jars down in a boiler with the lids, cover with cold water, then cover with a lid. Bring to the boil over high heat and boil the jars for 20 minutes.

(3) Stand the jars upright, without touching each other, on a wooden board on the lowest oven shelf. Turn the oven to the lowest possible temperature; leave jars to heat for 30 minutes.

Remove jars from the oven or dishwasher with a tea towel, or from the boiling water with tongs and rubber-gloved hands; the water will evaporate from hot wet jars quite quickly. Stand jars upright, and not touching each other, on a wooden board or a bench covered with a tea towel. Fill jars as directed in the recipe; secure the lids tightly, holding jars firmly with a tea towel or an oven mitt. Leave the jars at room temperature to cool before storing.

stock
beef intensely flavoured liquid made by simmering beef bones in water to extract the flavour.
chicken intensely flavoured liquid made by simmering chicken bones in water to extract the flavour.
vegetable intensely flavoured liquid made by simmering vegetables in water to extract the flavour.

sugar
brown soft, finely granulated sugar retaining molasses for its characteristic colour and flavour.
caster also known as superfine or finely granulated table sugar.
dark brown moist, dark brown sugar with a rich distinctive full flavour coming from natural molasses syrup.
icing (confectioners') also called powdered sugar; pulverised granulated sugar crushed together with a small amount of cornflour (cornstarch).

sugar snaps also called honey snap peas; fresh small peas which can be eaten whole, pod and all.

sumac purple-red, astringent spice ground from berries growing on shrubs flourishing wild around the Mediterranean; adds a tart, lemony flavour to food. Available from supermarkets.

sweet potato vegetable sometimes known as kumara.

tarragon leaves small slender leaf with a mild aniseed or licorice flavour.

thai basil is also known as horapa; different from holy basil and sweet basil in both look and taste, featuring smaller leaves and purplish stems. It has a slight aniseed taste and is one of the identifying flavours of Thai food.

thyme basic herb of French cuisine widely used in Mediterranean countries to flavour meats and sauces. A member of the mint family, it has tiny grey-green leaves that give off a pungent minty, light-lemon aroma.

tofu also known as soy bean curd or bean curd; an off-white, custard-like product made from the 'milk' of crushed soy beans.

tomato
canned whole peeled tomatoes in natural juices; available crushed, chopped or diced. Use undrained.
cherry also called tiny tim or tom thumb tomatoes; small and round.
chutney condiment made from tomatoes, vinegar and spices.
passata sieved tomato puree. To substitute, puree and sieve canned tomatoes or use canned tomato puree, which is similar but slightly thicker.
paste triple-concentrated tomato puree used to flavour soups, stews and sauces.
roma (egg) also called plum, these are smallish, oval-shaped tomatoes much used in Italian cooking or salads.
semi-dried semi-dried, partially dried tomato pieces in olive oil; softer and juicier than sun-dried, these are not a preserve, thus do not keep as long as sun-dried.

tortillas thin, round unleavened bread originating in Mexico. Two kinds are available, one made from wheat flour and the other from corn.

turmeric also called kamin; is a rhizome related to galangal and ginger. Must be grated or pounded to release its acrid aroma and pungent flavour. Fresh turmeric can be substituted with the more commonly found dried powder (proportions are 1 teaspoon of ground turmeric for every 20g of fresh turmeric).

unsalted butter often used in baking because it does not contain any salt, which may tend to alter the flavour of the food when added to some recipes.

vanilla
extract made by extracting the flavour from the vanilla bean pod; the pods are soaked, usually in alcohol, to capture an authentic vanilla flavour.
paste made from vanilla beans and contains real seeds. Is highly concentrated and 1 teaspoon replaces an entire vanilla bean.

vinegar
apple cider made from fermented apples.
balsamic originally from Modena, Italy, there are now many balsamic vinegars, ranging in pungency and quality depending on how, and for how long, they have been aged. Quality can be determined up to a point by price; use the most expensive sparingly.
red wine made from red wine.
white wine made from white wine.

watercress one of the cress family, a large group of peppery greens. Highly perishable, so must be used as soon as possible after purchase.

white miso paste fermented soybean paste. There are many types of miso, each with its own aroma, flavour, colour and texture. Can be refrigerated in an airtight container for up to a year. Generally, the darker the miso, the saltier the taste and denser the texture.

worcestershire sauce thin, dark-brown spicy sauce developed by the British when in India; used as a seasoning for meat, gravies and cocktails, and as a condiment.

yeast (dried or fresh) a raising agent used in dough-making. Granular (7g sachets) and fresh compressed (20g blocks) yeast can almost always be substituted one for the other.

zucchini also known as courgette; small green, yellow or white vegetable belonging to the squash family. When harvested young, its edible flowers can be stuffed then deep-fried or oven-baked.

INDEX

A
Apple berry crumble **156**

B
Beef and dark ale stew **110**
Beef Diane with mushrooms and peppercorns **108**
Beef in Guinness **120**
Beef ragu **106**
Beef, ricotta and spinach lasagne **122**
Butterscotch puddings with espresso caramel sauce **172**

C
Caramel macadamias **158**
Char sui and orange chicken pot roast **56**
Cheer up chicken soup **28**
Cheese and garlic mashed potato **146**
Chicken and borlotti bean soup **10**
Chicken and sweet corn soup **24**
Chicken cacciatore **44**
Chicken, chorizo and bean cassoulet **54**
Chicken cooked in wine with herbed dumplings **58**
Chicken korma **50**
Chicken, miso and soba noodle soup **22**
Chicken puff pies **48**
Chicken, rosemary and barley stew **60**
Chicken stew with grapes, pine nuts and agrodolce **46**
Chilli con lentil stuffed capsicums **126**
Chocolate tiramisu self-saucing pudding **170**
Classic chicken soup **14**
Creamy mashed potato **144**

F
Fall-apart ginger beer and rum beef ribs **118**
Flavoured mashed potatoes **146**
Fresh-baked herb bread **142**
Fried sage leaves **104**

G
Garlic-studded beef in red wine **114**
Ginger, chilli and pork dumpling soup **38**

H
Ham hock minestrone **18**
Hearty meat ragu with mixed mushrooms **104**
Hearty spiced carrot and lentil soup **30**
Homemade egg pasta **148**

I
Italian beef and barley soup with edible pastry spoons **32**
Italian beef casserole **100**
Italian beef sausage macaroni **116**
Italian bolognese **112**
Italian citrus, olive oil and polenta pudding **168**
Italian lamb shanks with lentils **82**

L
Lamb ragu with cherry tomatoes, rosemary and handkerchief pasta **66**
Lamb, vegetable and olive stew **70**
Lamb with peas and mint **78**
Leftover pot pies **80**
Leftovers soup **180**
Lemonade scones **166**
Lentil and eggplant ragu **132**

M
Massaman curry leg of lamb **72**
Mediterranean chicken **52**
Mexican pork with beans **90**
Middle Eastern eggplants **134**
Middle Eastern lamb **74**
Mini lamb pot pies **86**
Mini lamb shoulder roasts with butter beans **84**
Mulled wine **150**
Mushroom and lentil ragu **128**
Mustard mashed potato **146**

O
Osso buco with fennel, orange and gremolata **102**

Oven-roasted Middle Eastern cauliflower soup **36**
Overnight porridge **164**

P
Parmesan chips **18**
Parsley and lemon mashed potato **146**
Pea, ham and pesto soup **34**
Pine nuts and pesto mashed potato **146**
Pork, apple and cider stew with crispy potato **96**
Pork sausages with potatoes, onion and rosemary **94**
Pumpkin, carrot, lentil and ginger soup **16**

R
Red chicken curry **62**
Red wine and caramelised onion lamb shanks **76**
Ricotta, pesto and brown rice stuffed capsicums **130**
Rosé rhubarb sponge puddings **160**

S
Seafood soup with herb and garlic toasties **12**
Self-saucing sticky date and banana pudding **154**
Semolina dumplings **100**
Simple chocolate cake **162**
Slow-cooked rosé rhubarb **158**
Slow-cooked tomato Napoletana sauce **140**
Slow-roasted Greek-style lamb shanks **68**
Smoky chicken, chickpea, tomato and chorizo soup **26**
Snazzy couscous **74**
Soup toppers **182**
Spinach and ricotta cannelloni **136**

T
Thai-style pork **92**
Thai sweet potato soup with prawn skewers **40**

V
Vegetable and barley soup **20**

CONVERSION CHART

MEASURES

One Australian metric measuring cup holds approximately 250ml; one Australian metric tablespoon holds 20ml; one Australian metric teaspoon holds 5ml.

The difference between one country's measuring cups and another's is within a two- or three-teaspoon variance and will not affect your cooking results. North America, New Zealand and the United Kingdom use a 15ml tablespoon.

All cup and spoon measurements are level. The most accurate way of measuring dry ingredients is to weigh them. When measuring liquids, use a clear glass or plastic jug with the metric markings.

We use extra-large eggs with an average weight of 60g each.

DRY MEASURES

metric	imperial
15g	½oz
30g	1oz
60g	2oz
90g	3oz
125g	4oz (¼lb)
155g	5oz
185g	6oz
220g	7oz
250g	8oz (½lb)
280g	9oz
315g	10oz
345g	11oz
375g	12oz (¾lb)
410g	13oz
440g	14oz
470g	15oz
500g	16oz (1lb)
750g	24oz (1½lb)
1kg	32oz (2lb)

LIQUID MEASURES

metric	imperial
30ml	1 fluid oz
60ml	2 fluid oz
100ml	3 fluid oz
125ml	4 fluid oz
150ml	5 fluid oz
190ml	6 fluid oz
250ml	8 fluid oz
300ml	10 fluid oz
500ml	16 fluid oz
600ml	20 fluid oz
1000ml (1 litre)	1¾ pints

LENGTH MEASURES

metric	imperial
3mm	⅛in
6mm	¼in
1cm	½in
2cm	¾in
2.5cm	1in
5cm	2in
6cm	2½in
8cm	3in
10cm	4in
13cm	5in
15cm	6in
18cm	7in
20cm	8in
22cm	9in
25cm	10in
28cm	11in
30cm	12in(1ft)

OVEN TEMPERATURES

The oven temperatures featured with the recipes in this book are provided for both conventional and fan-forced ovens

	°C (Celsius)	°F (Fahrenheit)
Very slow	120	250
Slow	150	300
Moderately slow	160	325
Moderate	180	350
Moderately hot	200	400
Hot	220	425
Very hot	240	475

The imperial measurements used in these recipes are approximate only. Measurements for cake pans are approximate only. Using same-shaped cake pans of a similar size should not affect the outcome of your baking. We measure the inside top of the cake pans to determine sizes.

are
media *books*

Published in 2021 by **Are Media Books**, Australia.
Are Media Books is a division of Are Media Pty Limited.

ARE MEDIA
Chief Executive Officer Brendon Hill

ARE MEDIA BOOKS
General Manager, Publishing Sally Eagle
Editorial & Food Director Sophia Young

BETTER HOMES AND GARDENS
Editor Dora Papas
Creative Director Scott Cassidy
Deputy Editor Artemis Gouros
Chief Sub Editor Lisa Chant
Food Editor Sarah Murphy
Operations Manager David Scotto
Business Development Manager
Simone Aquilina Ph +61 2 8268 6278
simone.aquilina@aremedia.com.au

SLOW COOKING + COMFORT FOOD
Recipes Elle Vernon
Art Director Dania Smith Warmerdam
Photography Andre Martin, Pablo Martin
Styling Stephanie Souvlis, Annette Forrest, Jane Collins, Sarah O'Brien, Elle Vernon
Food Prep Kayla Cameron, Jennene Plummer, Mandy Sinclair, Elle Vernon

facebook.com/BHGaus Instagram @bhgaus

Printed in China by
Leo Paper Products LTD.
A catalogue record for this book is available from the National Library of Australia.
ISBN 978-1-92586-655-1 (hardback)
© Are Media Pty Ltd 2021 ABN 18 053 273 546